I CAN DO ANYTHING IN THE RIGHT PAIR OF SHOES

WALKING IN PEACE IN A TURBULENT WORLD

DR. NATALIE ATWELL

I Can Do Anything in the Right Pair of Shoes —
Copyright ©2024 by Dr. Natalie Atwell

Published by UNITED HOUSE Publishing

All rights reserved. No portion of this book may be reproduced or shared in any form–electronic, printed, photocopied, recording, or by any information storage and retrieval system, without prior written permission from the publisher. The use of short quotations is permitted.

ESV: The ESV Global Study Bible®, ESV® Bible, Copyright © 2012 by Crossway, All rights reserved.

New American Standard Bible (NASB): Scripture quotations taken from the (NASB®) New American Standard Bible®, Copyright © 1960, 1971, 1977 by The Lockman Foundation. Used by permission. All rights reserved. lockman.org

New International Version (NIV): Scripture quotations marked (NIV) are taken from the Holy Bible, New International Version®, NIV®. Copyright © 1973, 1978, 1984, 2011 by Biblica, Inc.™ Used by permission of Zondervan. All rights reserved worldwide. www.zondervan.com. The "NIV" and "New International Version" are trademarks registered in the United States Patent and Trademark Office by Biblica, Inc.™ or Scripture quotations taken from The Holy Bible, New International Version® NIV®, Copyright © 1973, 1978, 1984, 2011 by Biblica, Inc.™, Used by permission. All rights reserved worldwide.

ISBN: 978-1-952840-49-4

UNITED HOUSE Publishing
Waterford, Michigan
info@unitedhousepublishing.com
www.unitedhousepublishing.com

Photography:
Karen Gofoth

Interior design:
Matt Russell, Marketing Image, mrussell@marketing-image.com

Printed in the United States of America
2024—First Edition

SPECIAL SALES
Most UNITED HOUSE books are available at special quantity discounts when purchased in bulk by corporations, organizations, and special-interest groups. For information, please e-mail orders@unitedhousepublishing.com

*I dedicate this book to my parents,
Mike and Brenda Roper, who
taught me how to put on peace
by walking with Jesus daily.*

This is a book for all generations! It will help anyone who desires to walk in the peace that only Christ can give. Dr. Atwell reveals just how anyone can truly do anything in the right shoes, as she authentically uses her own physical handicap (born with severely clubbed feet) and paints an amazing picture of Scriptural truth in brilliant colors that inspire us all.

- David & Jason Benham
Best-Selling Authors,
Nationally-Acclaimed Entrepreneurs

A powerful story that can help others find peace in turbulent times...anchored in Christ!

- Dr. Tim Clinton
President,
American Association of Christian Counselors

Dr. Natalie Atwell's "I Can Do Anything in the Right Pair of Shoes" is a delightful and thoughtful journey through a most unique perspective... your shoe choice...all guided by a licensed counselor with a knack for wit and wisdom. Through clever anecdotes, sound advice, and a dash of humor, Dr. Atwell empowers women to navigate life's varied terrains with confidence and style. Packed with rich examples and backed by scripture, this book is not only compelling but also spiritually enriching. A must-read for anyone seeking guidance, inspiration, and a good laugh along the way.

- Dar Draper
President,
The GLOW Mission

We spend the majority of our lives wearing shoes. How they look and fit matters. In this book, Dr. Natalie Atwell draws from years of professional counseling experience to craft a compelling and creative description of the different styles of shoes we may be wearing, and how having the God-perspective can order our steps into His shalom for our lives no matter what things may have handicapped or shaped us.

- Jay Stewart
Pastor/Author

I am so grateful for Dr. Natalie's impact and influence in the life of my family. I truly believe you'll be so blessed by the life experiences and insight she brings on the pages of this wonderful book.

- Mike Weaver
Singer/songwriter of award-winning Christian band, Big Daddy Weave and author of I am redeemed.

There are books that coddle people in their captivity and then there are books that give tools to help people break free. This book is the latter. Dr. Atwell's stories are captivating, her insights are fresh, and, frankly, the Holy Spirit is in this book. I believe Dr. Atwell carries an anointing to truly help people break the chains of their past in order to fully seize their future. If you are ready to shed the negativity of your past, embrace your destiny, and live the life you were meant to live, then this book is for you!

- Dr. Douglas Witherup
Global Senior Pastor of the Multiply Family of Churches, professor, and author

Contents

PART ONE | Finding Peace with Your Past 7
ONE Bars and Braces That Shape Us—Reflections on the Past 9
TWO Sunday Best—Discovering Beliefs That Define Us. 23
THREE Patent Leather—Evaluating the Imprints Formed in Childhood... 37

PART TWO | Fighting the Enemy with Peace in the Present 53
FOUR The Cinderella Squeeze—Good vs. Bad Comparison 55
FIVE Loafers—Letting Go of Comforts. 67
SIX Shoes as a "Push Present"—Preparing for the Unexpected 81
SEVEN The High Heel Weapon—Navigating Conflicts 95
EIGHT Go-to Shoes—Considering Your Relationships 109
NINE Purple Hologram Shoes—Living in an Overstimulated World ... 125
TEN Interview Shoes—Avoiding Dangerous Distractions. 137
ELEVEN Personalized—Stop Making Everything about Me 149

PART THREE | Finding Peace with Your Future 163
TWELVE Red Soles—Developing a Healthy Outlook 165
THIRTEEN The Collector's Item—Looking for Lessons Along the Way. . 181
FOURTEEN Jesus' Shoes—Choosing Peace Every Day. 197

Notes. 211
Acknowledgements 219
About the Author 223

PART ONE

Finding Peace with Your Past

*"Scars have the strange power to
remind us that our past is real."*

— Cormac McCarthy, author,
All the Pretty Horses[1]

ONE

Bars and Braces That Shape Us—Reflections on the Past

I've always been a handful as we say here in the south of the USA. Most who know me well would agree that I've always been full of adventure and surprise. Mom said it started the day I was born.

Have you ever had one of "those doctor appointments" that starts out as a normal checkup and ends with you being sent to the hospital? This is how my introduction to the world began. Mom went for a normal checkup and when the doctor realized how much pain she was in, to the hospital she was sent.

Both of my parents have a high pain tolerance. For almost forty years, my dad worked for the Air National Guard. Once while he was helping prepare a plane and crew to depart, he decided to place an encouraging gospel track in a co-worker's bag. As he stooped down, a different co-worker ran over him with a truck because he didn't see him. This resulted in Dad having to be rushed to the hospital to have his spleen removed while also dealing with other injuries. I like to call Dad "road kill" because of this story.

I was my mom's third pregnancy which may make one think this is why she had a high tolerance for the pain, but her first pregnancy was a better indicator as she went into full blown labor and didn't know it. Dad called the doctor but he basically told her to go back to bed so she tried until bleeding started. Dad then took her to the hospital where she shortly thereafter delivered my twin sisters at 7 months.

My parents may have developed a high emotional pain tolerance from enduring family hardships as adolescents, but nothing could have prepared them for losing the twins the day they were born. Thankfully, beauty became ashes as their death led to my dad's decision to follow Jesus and they were given another daughter. My older sister, Jessica was healthy and strong, so my parents were hopeful that I would be too.

Arguably, my parents could have been considered prepared for just about anything.

However, when the doctor came to show me to my dad and family, he didn't exactly have a look of excitement on his face. I was wrapped up in the doctor's arms as expected, but my dad said he could tell, by the look on the doctor's face, something was wrong . . . and so the adventure began.

Mom doesn't remember learning anything about my feet or even seeing them until her doctor came in with an orthopedic doctor. They informed my mom my feet were severely clubbed, and my feet were fitted into casts right away. My left foot was laid against my leg and had no heel, and the right foot was turned in toward the other. My parents never saw my feet before the casts were put on. I can't imagine not being able to see the feet of my own precious baby. As a mother, one of the first things I wanted to see were my babies' feet. Although their feet aren't nearly as cute now, I still thank God for their feet and the fact that they are basically perfect.

In the hospital nursery, my mom said I woke up every couple of hours, screaming a frightening cry, most likely because of the pain I was in, as my feet were being forced into new positions. When my parents took me home, reacting to my anxious and frightening cries, my dad held me all night in the recliner. I still become teary-eyed when I think of my dad holding me through my pain. There is no doubt in my mind it was his warm, comforting hold that prevented me from long-lasting trauma related to this time. Touch has been proven to help people heal faster, and I believe my father's touch definitely aided in my healing as a child.

After a long night, Dad took me back to have my casts changed the next day. The sound of the saw cutting off the casts terrified me, as you can imagine. Mom and Dad, from that point on, had to deal with a newborn in casts and ongoing surgeries, starting when I was two months old. The cute pajamas didn't fit, the onesies with feet sewn in weren't an option, and back then, they didn't make the cute baby gowns like they do today. However, during the daytime, Mom made sure to dress me in the most adorable dresses she could find.

I didn't walk within my first year or so as most children do, and there were no shoes to go along with the casts that covered my entire legs and feet. But, from what I was told, I was a heck of a scooter! Thank God, this didn't become my nickname. My crazy, strong-willed, amazing grandmother and her family worked in the furniture business, so she had her nephew, Ralph Jr., make me a board with wheels on it so I could get around a bit easier. My strong will developed during my toddler years, as I had to work harder than most kids my age to move around.

Parents may wonder when children can remember their first memories in detail. Multiple studies have shown the importance of holding infants, the impact of proper sleeping, instilling good eating patterns in your children, promoting social/emotional development among toddlers, and more. We know everything we do for babies and toddlers is extremely important and memorable, but no one knows at what age children can reflect and describe, with detail, events that have happened to them.

I CAN DO ANYTHING IN THE RIGHT PAIR OF SHOES

Arguably, this could be related to the unique design of each individual by our Creator. The process of timing or remembering is different for each of us. Without a doubt, one of my first vivid memories was when I was two years old and taken back to surgery in a "crib" hospital bed. As a two-year-old, I felt like I was in a mobile prison cell being taken to a torture chamber. This sounds intense, but I can still remember the strong feelings of fear as I reflect on this time. I remember screaming bloody murder, as we say in the South, in hopes someone would rescue me. The skill I developed later on in life to scream (not literally, now) or to fight and figure out how to get help for myself and others may have begun at this moment.

It has been said in an old proverb that necessity is a great teacher. I would agree. I thought I had to fight for someone to hear me at that moment, and I was not giving up. The story told by my mother is that my screaming, crying, and fighting were so intense that it took them longer than normal to calm me enough to give me anesthesia. My childhood pastor, Preacher Parker, my Aunt Dianne, and my mom were all crying because they could hear my screams, yet couldn't rescue me. This breaks my heart to think of how helpless they must have felt.

My first shoes didn't come until after my second birthday when I was fitted for ones that were boot-looking and had braces. Each one had a bar connected that was extremely uncomfortable and somewhat painful. My mom said that no matter how they finagled those shoes, I could always wiggle out of them. Dad recently told me, he would pick me up at times by the bars attached to my shoes to play with me. Mom believes my dad shaking me around could be why I'm so silly now.

After two more surgeries (ages five and sixteen), multiple physical scars, and many memories, years later, God has given me the ability to not only walk but to run. Learning with shoes that had braces and bars was how I began walking in life.

Bars and Braces That Shape Us—Reflections on the Past

While the braces helped me, as did the bars, the bars often felt more like hindrances.

At times, God gives me analogies like the braces and bars analogy to help others and myself relate to and explain things. Likely because of my struggle and now admiration of shoes, I love that God chose shoes as the part of His armor that represents the gospel of peace. To get to a place of being able to walk in the shoes of peace daily, we need to begin by reflecting on our past, to make peace with it, so the enemy can't use it against us anymore! Satan uses our past against us as a way of attacking us from behind. The shoes in the Roman armor, described in Ephesians 6, had spikes in them to keep feet firmly planted, in case of an attack from behind.

An analogy God showed me about our past is relating memories to braces and bars. The braces are the positive things in our lives that were there with us during difficult times. Bars are the things that held us back, or are still holding us back, from moving on in life. Can you think of something in your past that has held you back and kept you from walking in peace? While I had physical bars and braces growing up, there are other memories that, at times, have felt like bars in my past, which is why I'm so thankful for the braces God has given me, so I can walk in peace daily.

Shoes make me feel prepared for any activity, situation, meeting, race, or task, by providing support, style, and protection. Though my journey to be able to wear shoes was definitely painful—one that made me wonder for years how I was ever going to understand the Biblical teaching of wearing the feet or shoes of peace as a part of the armor of God (Ephesians 6:15, NLT), by the grace of God, I have developed a love for them to this day.

I CAN DO ANYTHING IN THE RIGHT PAIR OF SHOES

Bars

You may not have had literal bars in your past, but I'm sure you've experienced theoretical ones. Bars are something that obstructs or prevents passage, progress, or action. Bars of our past may include disabilities, divorce, abuse, natural disasters, accidents, being bullied, being rejected from a team or group, changing schools, being unemployed, infidelity, or trying drugs or other illegal substances—the list could go on.

Assuredly, when reflecting on our experiences and memories, it is tough to imagine finding peace with it all. Finding peace with your past is when you accept the pain, learn to understand some, if not all, aspects of it, and find resolve as you walk in the confidence of the Lord, no matter how turbulent the past was. Processing the pain associated with our "bars" is a step toward finding peace with our past. Three of the categories of bars I encourage you to consider, as you seek to find peace, are bars from traumatic experiences, bars from unresolved issues, and bars from unforgiveness. Do you have trauma, unresolved issues, or unforgiveness from your past preventing you from walking in peace?

1. Bars from traumatic experiences:

Most, if not all, people have experienced some type of trauma within their lifetime. Our past painful moments and traumatic experiences, left unresolved, can become bars that hold us back from true freedom and peace. I know it is difficult to think, let alone talk, about your pain buried in the past. However, after years as a Licensed Clinical Mental Health Counselor, treating others in a therapy setting, I know it is vital to finding peace. One important key to unlocking the bars from the past is to find someone you can trust to talk to, which could be a therapist/counselor, a pastor, or a friend. I can't tell you how often, after someone has disclosed excruciating memories with me, a client has said, "I feel so much better." The lie of the enemy is if you don't deal with it, the pain will magically disappear one day. It is a lie; it doesn't. The pain will eat away at you and potentially continue to harm you and those around you. In my experience of processing the trauma from my disability and other painful memories through counseling, meditating on Scripture, and allowing myself to be loved by others, God has not only healed my hurts but has used them to bring healing and inspiration to others.

2. Bars From Unresolved Issues:

Almost weekly, in my sessions, I give an analogy where I ask people to imagine pushing all of the dirt in their homes under a rug in their living room for years. Then, I ask them to imagine the pile eventually becoming a mountain that they begin bumping into daily. At some point, you can't even walk through the room. Unresolved issues pushed under our theoretical rugs do the same in our lives. Over time, our unresolved issues indirectly cause harm to our relationships, decisions, and other areas of our lives.

Your pile of dirt will not resolve itself, so let me encourage you to begin cleaning out the mess from under your rug. I will warn you that as you begin to clean out, you may feel discomfort. Just like cleaning under an old rug, it may cause you to sneeze at first, but, eventually, you'll adjust until it's all cleaned out. Then, if you clean it regularly, your relationships, and everything else in your life, will function better, and you can be healthier, useful, and ultimately, at peace.

3. Bars of Unforgiveness:

As you clean out, you may also find some areas in which you need to find forgiveness, either for yourself or others. I once heard it said that not forgiving someone is like swallowing rat poison and expecting it to kill the person you can't forgive. It actually kills you. Forgiveness doesn't mean what the other person did was right; it just means you forgive, so you can move on. It also doesn't mean you have to reconcile with the other person. Reconciliation can only happen if the other person acknowledges their wrongdoing and if you desire reconciliation to occur. Jesus died for and forgave all, but He is only reconciled to those who confess their sin and seek a relationship with Him.

There was an individual in my life who I had to forgive years ago. This person wrecked my family by sexually abusing multiple family members. I hated him. I dreamed of literally punching him if I ever saw him in person. My husband told me never to point him out in public for fear of what he might do to this man. As I studied forgiveness and learned more about the people in my life I needed to forgive, he was at the top of the list.

I did not want to forgive him; I wanted to throw my shoe at him, not put one of peace on! At times, I found much more comfort in the passage of scripture where God threw His shoe at Edom and crushed His enemies (Psalm 60:8). While I know God will cast His shoe over His enemies, I also know He died for all. So, when He asks us to put on the shoes of the gospel of peace, it is out of His forgiveness that we, too, can do so.

It was hard, but I forgave. Eventually, I got to the point where I could ride by the area where this person lived without feeling angry. Thankfully, God never called me to reconcile with this person. I admire people who do, but God doesn't call all to this end. I have found peace through forgiving this person. My friend, I want you to experience this peace too, so is there someone you need to forgive so you can walk in peace?

One of the ways I was able to find peace in forgiving is through seeking counseling. Through this process, I learned so many valuable things. For one, I realized I am a strong and protective mother because of what I went through. I'm not fearful, but you'd better believe I ask a lot of questions when my boys stay with other people. Also, I have learned that by sharing my story, many others felt comfortable enough with me to share their story.

As a therapist, when I look into the eyes of someone who has been sexually abused and say, "I know how you feel," and when I'm called to disclose some of my story to help a client, the result is always hope for the other person; hope that ultimately leads to peace.

One of my favorite quotes on forgiveness came from a story about a lady named Mary Johnson who forgave the man who murdered her son. In 1993, Mary's only son was murdered outside of Minneapolis, when he was only 20 years old. She thought, for years, that she had forgiven the man who killed her son because the Bible told her to, and she had said it, but she realized, at some point, she hadn't forgiven him in her heart. She realized the root of bitterness ran deep; she hated everyone and drove many people away, for years, until one day, she decided to go visit her son's murderer in prison. She said, "When he left the room I bent over saying – 'I've just hugged the man who murdered my son.' Then, as I got up, I felt something rising from the soles of my feet and leaving me. From that day on I haven't felt any hatred, animosity, or anger. It was over."[2]

We must also evaluate the things we should forgive ourselves for from our past. If Jesus died for us and His forgiveness is good enough, who are we not to forgive others and ourselves? Forgiveness is a step to walking in peace daily but definitely not an easy one. My desire is for you to have this feeling of bitterness and unforgiveness rising from the soles of your feet and leaving you too! This is truly a key to walking in peace. I know it is hard to do, but it will be worth it as you begin to feel the bitterness leave you. Part of the work is going back and realizing those who were there for you—the braces—

during the hard times.

Braces

Braces are those people, places, and things that are used to prepare, strengthen, and support you during challenging times. We all need these braces to put on our shoes of peace. My physical shoes had braces, and so did my shoes of peace! The brace can include family, friends, teachers, neighbors, godparents, etc. It could also include angels whom God has placed in our lives along the way to help us during difficult times. God Himself is a brace- the only one who promises to never leave or forsake us. We can walk in peace because He is with us. Finally, there is the brace of meditating on Scripture. Meditation has been proven to be very powerful. Meditate on the Bible, the Word of God.

1. The Brace of Others

People who were there along the way, in direct and indirect ways, are braces for your journey. There is an activity I do with my clients, from time to time, where I ask them to write down significant memories in five to ten-year increments and write down who was there for them during those times. Why don't you try this now?

Without fail, no matter how bad the situation or experience, they all list someone who was there- a parent, teacher, neighbor, elderly lady at church, social worker, stranger, or acquaintance who even just made them laugh during a tough time. If we all think long enough, someone was there. Maybe our "brace" couldn't rescue us at the moment, but he or she was there nonetheless. Reflecting on our "braces" is one step to finding peace with our past. It allows us to see the truth that God has never left us or forsaken us. He sent others to be with us.

2. The Brace of God

Along my journey, I have discovered that while God didn't originally design for me to have a birth defect, disability, or other painful moments in life, He will not waste the pain I've experienced. His plan, from the beginning, was for me to be made perfect in His image, walking with Him daily in the garden of Eden. But when man chose his own way, the world became cursed. Some people blame God or struggle with bitterness because of many things they were born with, born into, or that happened to them in childhood, but these are truly effects of the curse. I had to come to an understanding that my own birth defect, and other painful aspects of life, were simply a part of our broken and cursed world. Doing so has allowed me to also accept the truth that although bad things happen in this world, God is good, and the knowledge of this is a brace allowing me to put on the shoes of peace.

As I have sought to process my own trauma and allow God to be a brace, He has lovingly led me to Himself through others and also through Scripture. It may seem odd to some that, as I contemplate the things of God, I find strength in reading stories about others who struggle with physical disabilities. In 2 Samuel 4:4 (NASB), it states, "Now Jonathan, Saul's son, had a son who was disabled in both feet. He was five years old when the news of Saul and Jonathan came from Jezreel, and his nurse picked him up and fled. But it happened that in her hurry to flee, he fell and could no longer walk. And his name was Mephibosheth." Later on, King David wanted to show the kindness of God to the family of Saul, so he sent for Mephibosheth. In turn, David restored his family's inheritance. God didn't forget Mephibosheth.

I believe some of the details of this part of the story could have been left out, but God, in His divine revelation of Scripture, includes the details of Mephibosheth's feet. It shows me God remembers those who have struggles, whether physical or otherwise, and He loves them and provides for them. Many cultures at that time, and even now in certain parts of the world, treated people with physical disabilities as if they were the scum of the earth.

God has always been the support for the lowly or as I call it a brace. He is personal, relatable, and sovereign. I could choose to be bitter and blame God for allowing me to be born with clubbed feet, but instead, I look back and choose to see how God has been my brace during difficult times. Do you see God as a brace in your life? Have you allowed God to draw you into a deeper walk of peace with Him? Consider writing out your thoughts here.

3. The Brace of Scripture Through Meditation

Meditation is also a brace that can be used daily and can help make putting on our shoes of peace feel manageable. Meditating on Scripture keeps me grounded, motivated, challenged, and inspired. God often leads me to verses to pray over people and for myself as He guides me. You can use any verse God leads you to during a meditation exercise. Meditation helps to focus your mind, slow your anxious thoughts, and alleviate painful feelings. There are even stories of people who practice meditation and forgo anesthesia during surgery. Can you imagine? Could Jesus have been meditating on His love for us as He endured the pain and agony of the cross? It may seem like a strange practice, but it is worth a try to help you find peace with your past.

Letting Go of Bars and Being Thankful for the Braces

Finding peace with our past involves processing it, laughing at it, crying over it, and learning from it. Reflecting and asking God "why" can take us to a place of peace with our past, if we allow Him to reveal some of the reasons He

Bars and Braces That Shape Us—Reflections on the Past

has given blessings and struggles, and if we trust Him with the things He doesn't reveal. I could choose to stay bitter and live with a "disabled" mindset for my physical setbacks or my past painful memories, but instead, I walk in the peace of Christ and follow Him. John 8:12, NIV, says, "Jesus spoke to them, saying, 'I am the light of the world. Whoever follows me will not walk in darkness, but will have the light of life.'"

In part, the way to walk in light rather than darkness is by putting on the right shoes! Can you imagine going into rough terrain without shoes? Now, imagine facing the world each day without peace. Have you ever been going through the routine of a normal day and felt attacked, all of a sudden, out of nowhere, by something related to your past? We need to put on the shoes of peace so we can effectively prepare for the attacks of Satan from behind (our past). As you learn to deal with and let go of the bars of your past and celebrate the braces of others, God, and Scripture, you will soon be walking in peace because you will have prepared by putting on the right shoes!

Reflection Questions and Activities:

- Write down your theoretical bars (traumatic experiences, unresolved issues, and unforgiveness) and the feelings associated with each bar.

- Consider the braces God has given you (people who were there for you during easy/transitional/difficult times), and write down each one by name and how they were there for you.

- Write down verses that help you find peace when reflecting on your past. For example, I love to consider Revelation 21:5, "And he who was seated on the throne said, 'Behold, I am making all things new.'" Also, he said, "Write this down, for these words are trustworthy and true."

I can walk in peace by dealing with the bars and being thankful for the braces in my life!

TWO

Sunday Best—Discovering Beliefs That Define Us

"Listen to the people who love you. Believe that they are worth living for even when you don't believe it. Seek out the memories depression takes away and project them into the future..."
— Andrew Solomon,
The Noonday Demon: An Atlas of Depression[3]

You shall teach them diligently to your children, and shall talk of them when you sit in your house, and when you walk by the way, and when you lie down, and when you rise.
Deuteronomy 6:7, ESV

My mom didn't talk about shoes all day, every day, but one of the beliefs she taught me was to dress your best on Sundays. That's why she asked my dad to shine my shoes each Sunday. This isn't a belief that majorly impacted my life, but it impacted me nonetheless.

There are some strong beliefs, silly beliefs, and harmful beliefs we develop as we grow up. Some of the strong beliefs I developed were regarding my faith in Christ. Honestly, most of them growing up were about church attendance, church people, and those who didn't attend church. I was taught to go to church every time the doors were open. This, for me, meant not only Sunday morning, Sunday night, and Wednesday night, but also stopping by the church during the week with my dad to say hello to the staff or attending youth service on Monday nights.

Such beliefs likely developed before my relationship with Christ began. Anyone who grew up in church likely developed beliefs about the church and the people of God before they truly started a relationship with Jesus. This is important to note because those beliefs we develop impact our views, feelings, and emotions even now. I still sometimes feel bad about not going to church on Wednesday nights due to the beliefs I grew up with, and not necessarily out of conviction from the Holy Spirit. Do you have any of these types of beliefs?

Beyond beliefs about the church, I also developed beliefs about family. My mom's dad (I never knew him, so I can't call him grandfather) left my grandmother with all of the kids, no money, and a hard life. This impacted my mom so much that she raised all three of her daughters to "NEVER depend on a man." All three of us have an education beyond high school, good jobs, and can support ourselves financially. This isn't necessarily a negative belief, and it is one I respect and appreciate because I know the root cause. Because of this belief, it was never an issue for me to go back to work after having kids. It has never been an issue for me to work, period. Conversely, I have other friends whose moms stayed home with them, so they hold the belief that "moms should stay home with their children" close to their hearts and lives, such that this is what they do without asking if this is what God wants for them.

Stop, and think about your beliefs about work, parenting, marriage, friendship, church, money, time, etc. Consider writing them out in a journal or notebook. As you do, you'll find that many of them stem from your childhood or past in one way or another.

I see this not only in my personal reflections but also in that of my clients. Many of them struggle with work, marriage, parenting, etc., because of beliefs from their childhood. For example, one parent may believe her kids should get everything they want because they grew up poor, while the other parent may want to teach the kids financial responsibility because he learned this from his parents. These are just a few examples, but do you see now how much our beliefs from childhood impact us? At times, our beliefs hinder us from walking in peace.

As you begin to consider how your past or childhood beliefs impact those around you in positive or negative ways, I hope you'll consider the ones you should keep and the ones you should throw out or let go. Many of your beliefs are not harmful, but unless you *evaluate* your beliefs, you can't uncover the ones keeping you from walking in peace.

Identify and Evaluate Your Beliefs

Consider grabbing your journal or notebook, and continue writing. As you read the next section, identify and evaluate your beliefs using the following:

Identify your automatic thoughts:

Begin identifying your beliefs by writing down your automatic thoughts on a given day. Automatic thoughts are the ones that seem to just happen or come out of nowhere. For example, *I'm hungry, I need to call my mom, I don't like my co-workers*, etc. Contemplate what your thoughts are surrounding certain places and situations. Consider keeping a small notebook or journal with you, throughout your day, for a week, month, or however long you can commit, and write down thoughts that lead to your beliefs, as they come to mind. You could also sit down once a day and reflect by thinking about your routines, thoughts, stressors, unmet needs, or desires from the day. There are a variety of ways to begin identifying thoughts related to your beliefs. The key is to find what process will work for you. This process may take time, but be patient with yourself. It will be worth your time to uncover some of your negative beliefs by identifying your automatic thoughts.

Ask others what they think you believe about yourself:
Another step in the process of identifying harmful beliefs may include thinking about your past by involving others who were close to you in the past and the present. It can be very humbling to ask others tough questions about yourself, but again, it is worth the work if you want to walk in peace. The goal is to try to figure out where the beliefs came from and where they are rooted. If we can find the original roots, we can pull these negative beliefs up by the root, so they are gone forever.

Take Note of the Thoughts that are Actual Beliefs You Have.
Once you've identified your automatic thoughts that lead to beliefs, sort these into positive or negative. Leave the positive ones alone, as these are helping you walk in peace. The thoughts and beliefs we need to deal with are the negative ones.

Contemplate the Distortions in Your Thinking.
After the negative thoughts/beliefs are identified, you should start to identify any potential distortions in your thinking. Ask yourself, "Why do I think this way?" Consider the rules you've given yourself. Examine the emotions you experience surrounding the negative thoughts and beliefs. Next, consider how your distorted thinking impacts your relationships. Finally, are your thoughts creeping into your daily activities?

Classify Your beliefs.
As you look through your automatic thoughts and

begin to identify potential beliefs, some may be obvious, and some not so much. Just write down the beliefs that come to mind as you review your automatic thoughts. Also, write down the beliefs you have in general about family, friends, work, faith, health, mental health, etc.

After you have a good, working list of beliefs, separate the beliefs into three categories: beliefs about myself, beliefs about others, and beliefs about the world. As you do, begin to star or mark the potentially harmful ones. These are the ones you need to truly focus on getting rid of, as they impact your life negatively.

Evaluate Your Thoughts

Once you've written down your thoughts, read them, think about them, and make sure you are honest. You don't have to share them with anyone else, but write them down and evaluate them. I'll be vulnerable and go first.

Here is a glimpse into my crazy *thoughts* for the day: Why is my husband snoring? Should we call the doctor? I wish he didn't have to go to work so early. I wish he loved his job. I love my morning coffee and Jesus time in my prayer closet. I'm not a fan of my son coming in and interrupting this time. I need a minute to prepare for the boys. I have thirty minutes to do my workout and get Maddox out the door. The laundry needs to be started. What am I going to have for supper today? This is just the first hour of my day.

Next, I think: I need to listen to my news podcast, get the boys to school, pray with them, be kind to the girl whom we carpool with, and then start my workday. I need to accomplish a lot and be very productive so I can focus on my family later. Which friend do I need to check on today? How are my sisters and parents? I should send a text to my husband to let him know I'm thinking about him. I could use a nap right now.

I CAN DO ANYTHING IN THE RIGHT PAIR OF SHOES

I'm hungry, but I need to count my calories. Time to get the boys. This car-rider line sucks.

I need to finish laundry, make sure the house is clean and supper is done when my husband gets home. Have the boys finished their homework? Do they need to practice anything sports-wise, or do they have practice? Have the boys read their Bibles? Let's do a family devotion. I'm exhausted. I want to spend time with my husband. I'm sleepy. My kids need to go to bed.

Looking back on my automatic thoughts, can you see some of my beliefs coming out in my thoughts? Maybe you see that I value God, the Bible, myself, being productive, having a clean home, having a happy spouse, and raising my kids to be hard workers and to love God. You could also see I worry about my weight. Did you question why I feel the need to have everything clean and neat and maybe perfect? Did you think, why does she need to be so busy? Why does she need to keep her kids working hard and focused? Why didn't she stop to take a nap? She seems like a people pleaser. The questions and reactions you may have could potentially be endless after looking into my thoughts.

In evaluating my thoughts and being aware of my own beliefs, I can tell you where they come from. I saw my dad read his Bible every morning as he drank his coffee. My dad is also an amazing, godly man. I know reading his Bible every day made a difference. He even read devotions with us at night as kids. My mom was an extremely driven and motivated woman. She did a lot when my dad was deployed. She valued a clean home. She pushed us to do well in school and in anything we were involved in. My mom also cared about her appearance and weight, and in turn, I did and do. She wasn't pushy about it with us, but it still influenced me. My parents valued friendships and church.

Looking back, I see so many of my beliefs resulting

from the things my parents did, or at times, didn't do. These beliefs come out in my daily thoughts and behaviors. It's crazy and easy to see once automatic thoughts are written out. Now, it's your turn.

Consider what you thought about when you woke up this morning. What did you want to eat for the day, and how did you decide to eat that specific food? You can ask as few or as many questions as you would like. What physical thoughts are you having? What spiritual thoughts? How about thoughts surrounding your relationships? Also, consider thoughts that come as a result of activities you are engaged in (i.e. driving, etc.).

Beliefs About Yourself

Now, take a look at the list of beliefs you have about yourself. Are they mostly positive or negative? Are the beliefs realistic? Are these beliefs rooted in facts or feelings? Sadly, so many people believe they are bad, evil, losers, not good enough, incompetent, ugly, stupid, rotten at the core, unworthy, undeserving, abnormal, boring, flawed, or unlovable. If your beliefs indicate any of those things, your ability to walk in peace will be hindered. It can also be unhealthy to think too highly of oneself. What does God say about you? Your beliefs should be positive, realistic, and rooted in the truth of God's word. When you can begin to get your beliefs about yourself in line with God's word, you will be able to walk in peace.

Unhealthy Beliefs About Others

Now, mark the beliefs you hold about others. What do you believe about others? Are most of the people in your life untrustworthy, manipulative, or unhealthy, or are most of the people in your life amazing, completely trustworthy, always kind, better than you, etc.?

These questions are important to ask because, if you find yourself believing primarily negative things about others, you will struggle to develop healthy relationships. Similarly, believing everyone can be trusted or that everyone is kind can cause you to be taken advantage of. Our beliefs about others impact the health of our relationships with others, in turn, impacting our ability to walk in peace.

Unhealthy Beliefs About the World

Finally, it is necessary to contemplate our beliefs about the world. As you review your beliefs about the world, consider the assumptions you may be making. Do your beliefs assume the world is completely terrible, or do your beliefs show the world as being a Disney World fantasy?

Assuming only negative things about the world can lead to turmoil and negativity, which are the opposite of peace. Conversely, if you only see the world through rose-colored glasses, you will not be able to have a proper view of all circumstances and situations regarding life in this world. We must believe that, no matter what, peace can exist regardless of the good or bad within the world.

Examples of Common Negative Beliefs People Have About Themselves, Others, and the World

The beliefs and values we were taught, and often the ones we caught, can be like boulders in the way of our voyage to find peace. Discovering even ten harmful core beliefs and uncovering where they came from can help us unlock the path to peace.

Sunday Best—Discovering Beliefs That Define Us

Self/Others:

- I can't change. I'll always be this way. I've always been this way. I'm helpless. *Focus on the truth. Change is a part of life. You can change. Don't believe the lie that you have to stay where you are.*

- People are too busy to help me or be with me. People don't like me. *Keep searching; some kind people will help you in the world. Pray for them to come along.*

- No one has a family as crazy as mine. I am unlovable. *Believe the truth that God loves you even when you don't feel it.*

- I'll never be satisfied until_____, or _____ will never happen. I am incompetent. *You were created for a plan and purpose. You will be competent in what God calls you to do.*

- People only like/love me based on what I can do for them. Otherwise, I am a burden. *Focus on why God created you. You are loved by God not for anything you do.*

- I have _____ (anxiety, depression, learning struggles, etc.). I define myself by my struggles. I am worthless. *You are who God says you are. You were fearfully and wonderfully made.*

- I don't deserve to be . . . (healthy, happy, financially stable). I am undeserving. *God sent his son to die for us even when we were undeserving. Thank God, even if you feel undeserving, use your gifts for good.*

- I can change him/her. *You can only change yourself. Let God change others.*

- My story isn't that great; therefore, I have nothing great to share or offer. *You are a part of God's story, the greatest story ever.*

- Nothing amazing happens to me. I am insignificant. *Do*

not let how the world defines significance be how you define it. You are significant, you are loved, and you are valued by the King of Kings and the God above all!

The World:
- The world is all going to hell in a handbasket. *There is still some good in the world. Look for it.*
- The world is all evil. *The world is not ALL evil. God is still here.*
- The world is out to get me. *This is a negative thought that will lead you nowhere.*
- The World will end on this exact date . . . *No man knows the day or time when the Lord will return to create a new heaven and earth.*
- We should hate the world/earth. *We should hate the "things of the world," not the world itself. We hate the sinful things.*
- The world is unfair. *Again, a negative thought will lead you nowhere. Whether this is true or not is not helpful, just keep going...*
- The world is full of hate. *There is still a lot of love. God's people should show more love!*
- The world is a terrible place to live. *Make it better! You have the power to overcome!*
- Life on Mars may be better. *Really?*
- Heaven can never happen on earth. *We can have a part of heaven on earth as we love others.*

Silly beliefs:
- You fall into love. *Instead, love is a choice.*
- We must eat dinner around the table. *Spend time togeth-*

- er weekly, no matter where it is.
- My family needs to be just like their family if it is good. *Focus on your traditions and values as a family.*
- I have to dress up to buy groceries. *No one cares what you look like in the store.*
- Church is done one way. Go to your husband's church; stay in a dying church or for family. *Get out of your comfort zone.*
- Ditzy is dumb. *Who doesn't love Phoebe on Friends?*
- You have to get married. *Single doesn't mean you haven't arrived. Plenty of people in the Bible were single like Paul.*
- You have to "like" everything. *Stop focusing on "likes", just look at social media occasionally; do what is natural.*
- Post your life. *Live your life.*
- Pepper makes you pretty. *Maybe it does.*
- Peanut butter is brain food. *It is protein.*
- My worth = How tidy, how decorated my house is, and how well-behaved my kids are. *If you don't have Jesus, nothing else matters.*
- Step on the crack, and you'll break your mom's back. *I've never found this to be true.*
- Perfection trumps obedience . . . Our obedience to the Lord only counts if executed with perfection. *This is SO far from the truth of grace and surrender to Him. Our obedience is what reaps a reward . . . not our perfectionism.*
- Popularity matters. *No; kindness matters.*
- Your choices as a pastor's kid will bring reproach to

your family. *They might, but others need to focus on their own lives instead of yours.*

- People will only accept me if I do something for them. *Sometimes this is true, but these shouldn't be "your people."*
- Drinking is the devil's dishwater. *Um . . . Jesus turned water into wine as his first miracle. Just don't be drunk with it!*

How to Overcome and Reframe: Identify the Past, then Change.

If we have negative views of others, we may think of them as untrustworthy, wishing to hurt us, demeaning, uncaring, or manipulative. Negative beliefs often cause us to constantly seek the approval of others, which is exhausting and doesn't lead to a peaceful life.

If our core beliefs are positive and helpful, we need to take no further action. If they are not, we must seek to transform them because limiting core beliefs are the root cause of low self-esteem. They shape how we treat ourselves, others, and even how others may treat us. They set the rules by which we live and the tone of our self-talk.

When our experiences do not align with our core beliefs, our minds, always set on avoiding cognitive dissonance, will twist them until they do.

Once you've identified and evaluated your negative beliefs, the next phase is to reframe your thoughts and beliefs about your past into new positive, truthful ones. We do this by memorizing scripture and hiding God's word in our hearts. To walk in peace, you need to have your beliefs about the world filtered through God's truth in scripture.

Sunday Best—Discovering Beliefs That Define Us

Here are some scriptures to begin memorizing to help transform your beliefs:

Do not be conformed to this world, but be transformed by the renewal of your mind, that by testing you may discern what is the will of God, what is good and acceptable and perfect.
Romans 12:2, ESV

Do not love the world or the things in the world. If anyone loves the world, the love of the Father is not in him. For all that is in the world—the desires of the flesh and the desires of the eyes and pride in possessions—is not from the Father but is from the world. And the world is passing away along with its desires, but whoever does the will of God abides forever.
1 John 2:15-17, ESV

I have said these things to you, that in me you may have peace. In the world, you will have tribulation. But take heart; I have overcome the world.
John 16:33, ESV

Ye are of God, little children, and have overcome them: because greater is he that is in you than he that is in the world.
1 John 4:4, ESV

For whatsoever is born of God overcometh the world: and this is the victory that overcometh the world, even our faith. Who is he that overcometh the world, but he that believeth that Jesus is the Son of God?
1 John 5:4-5, KJV

I CAN DO ANYTHING IN THE RIGHT PAIR OF SHOES

Activity: Cognitive Behavioral Therapy Technique

Cognitive Behavioral Therapy is an evidence-based approach that can be used to transform your negative thoughts into positive ones. As you practice this repeatedly, you will begin, automatically, thinking more positively or at least switching your negative thoughts into positive ones. Below is a simple activity to use from Cognitive Behavioral Therapy.

Write down your thoughts/beliefs in one column, and write the truth next to it. Repeat daily, and as often as needed, until you begin to notice you are automatically thinking more positively.

Examples:

I am not very smart → I will focus on being wise.

I am not wanted → God says I am fearfully and wonderfully made.

I can walk in peace by reframing negative beliefs about my past into new positive beliefs.

THREE

Patent Leather—Evaluating the Imprints Formed in Childhood

"I had removed my patent leather shoes after a while, for they foundered badly in the sand. It pleased me to think they would be perched there on the silver log, pointing out to sea, like a sort of soul-compass, after I was dead."
— Sylvia Plath, writer, *The Bell Jar*[4]

Patent leather was created in the late 1700s as a way to make leather waterproof. The name comes from the method being patented by the inventor. A patent is something that makes an exclusive or proprietary claim, according to Merriam-Webster.[5] Consider all of the patents people are likely seeking or have been attained in the past. If you were an inventor or creator, and you made something magnificent, you'd likely seek to obtain a patent on your creation so you could have a proprietary claim.

God is our creator and, therefore, should be given the patent to our lives. He gives us the gift of free will, which can lead our enemy to seek patents on our lives in different areas. The devil likes to attain patents on our self-esteem, trust, confidence, motivation, and resilience. He takes what was meant for good and twists, distorts, and seeks to ruin.

You may feel discouraged that an imprint from childhood has handicapped you in some way forever. My friend, the great news about imprints is that they can change. Jesus said in John 16:33 (ESV), "I have said these things to you, that in me you may have peace. In the world, you will have tribulation. But take heart; I have overcome the world." With Jesus, we can overcome our past and learn to walk in peace. Our imprints do not have to define us, and we can shine for Jesus, regardless of our hurts, just like my dad made my patent leather shoes shine on Sundays. As we learn to walk in peace by putting on the right shoes, God's peace will protect us from the enemy, much like patent leather is waterproofed for protection.

What are Imprints, and How Do They Impact Us?

Imprinting is learning that occurs during a specific and limited period in an animal's life, usually shortly after birth. Although imprinting can involve any type of learning, it is most commonly associated with bonding and developing relationships.[6] A visual representation of an imprint could be the idea of a stamp or a tattoo. There are different definitions for imprints, but for this chapter, I define an imprint as a belief that is developed from a deeply embedded memory. This memory often changes the way you view yourself, others, or the world. The memory becomes an imprint as it leaves a picture of the memory that is stored inside of you.

An imprint can be positive or negative. A positive imprint can develop into a good self-concept. However, negative imprints, that are not processed properly, can develop into irrational fears that can become personal truths. Negative imprints create erratic or illogical behavior since they are rooted in memories and not your present reality.

Some suggest many, if not all, imprints are in place by age seven, since the first critical development of the brain concludes around that time. This is why many child psychologists suggest maximizing this period by helping children embrace learning, focus on emotional learning, and engage in a diversity of experiences.[7]

You may outgrow some of the negative imprints you've developed such as negative beliefs about your physical appearance or negative beliefs about church (the list could go on). However, if you don't outgrow your past negative imprints, they can hinder you from growing in certain areas of your life. To ensure this doesn't happen, let's dive a little deeper into the topic so we can explore ways to release them from negatively impacting you.

Imprints can be categorized or related to physical well-being (genetic problems or other health problems), mental well-being (childhood trauma, mental illness, negative mindsets, or psychological problems), social well-being (relationships, community issues, or societal issues), and/or spiritual well-being (finding one's life purpose or meaning).

Whether or not you believe imprints are in place by age seven, they must be dealt with to find peace in the present—especially the negative ones. Processing your memories takes time, but it is worth it. It also can and should happen over time, not in one sitting.

Some of My Imprints

My first physical imprint was my clubfoot, which led me to feel self-conscious about my feet and legs since they are different sizes. It impacts me every day of my life and always has. As a kid, it was not being able to wear the shoes others could wear. As a teenager, it was insecurity. I thought guys wouldn't like me because my calves were different sizes. I still hate when people ask me questions about my feet or legs. Just writing this makes me a little anxious, thinking about how those who read this or hear my story may look at me differently, or at least my feet or legs.

I CAN DO ANYTHING IN THE RIGHT PAIR OF SHOES

As a little girl, I had to wear special shoes. I can remember the pictures with those shoes. I looked sad in the pictures; though I don't remember feeling sad at the time. As I grew and started playing dress up with friends, it was awkward, at times, when my feet just didn't fit into certain shoes. I loved to dress up in high heels and often fell, which led to constant bruises and scrapes on my legs. This could have happened to any little girl, but it felt like it happened to me more often.

Beyond my disability, I have also had to process other imprints. I'll never forget when a family member said I was chubby (imprint), when I was in fourth grade, and that she hoped I'd grow out of it. To this day, I still struggle, at times, with my body image; especially if someone comments about my legs or feet being different sizes. I hate when little girls are told negative things about their bodies, and I now help counsel girls who've dealt with the same imprint.

After being the baby of the family with a disability for almost seven years, I remember asking a pediatrician to take my baby sister back to where she came from. The imprint here was, *I am not going to be loved as I once was; I will always be second best.* It could have been the thought that my parents' attention was diverted out of necessity, not out of favoritism. The enemy tried to put a wedge between us from day one, but thankfully, my parents always taught us to be one another's best friends as sisters. I love my baby sister dearly now, but I endured a great deal of change during this time, including changing schools and moving. Do you ever wonder what your life would be like had something *not* taken place? Without my little sister, I may have grown up to be a total brat, or worse, a narcissist. Are there tough family relationships in your life that you need to look back at to assess some of the imprints that were created?

When my cousin died of AIDS when I was about eight

years old, I remember saying to myself I would never try drugs (imprint). Thankfully, I haven't to this day. He contracted AIDS from dirty needles and died at age twenty-two. I'm glad my parents didn't shield me from the truth because this imprint created a positive response in me. This imprint has caused me to speak the truth in love to my children, no matter how ugly the truth is. Can you imagine, though, if I had allowed the enemy to take this imprint and turn it into something negative such as, "My family is full of drug addicts, so I might as well be one." Or what if the enemy had tricked me into believing it was harmful to talk about these things with my kids instead of warning them of dangers? We can experience victory each time we overcome and allow God to be glorified when positive imprints in our lives take root instead of negative ones.

I also have memories from my childhood related to friendships that impacted me positively or negatively. I can remember the crushes I had in middle and high school and specific memories related to the guys I liked. I also remember the night my older sister told everyone I'd "entered womanhood." The older guys in the youth group told me, "Welcome to womanhood, Natalie." I was mortified. The imprint here was that *my older sister would always be better than me or prettier or not as stupid/young/immature.* Thankfully, I can laugh about this memory now . . . I'm sure she has plenty of imprinted memories of me, as well, like the time I chased her down to give her chickenpox.

I'll never forget a time in high school when I had a personal accident, and this mean girl told everyone about it. It was an incident of bullying. *Imprint: People want to make fun of me.* This caused me to be a strong advocate against bullying when I worked as a school counselor. I'll never forget a student I had who was made to lick the toilet seat in the boys' bathroom every day during lunch. When he told me, I made sure the school administrators did something about it that day because, in a way, I knew how he felt.

Of course, I have many imprints that were funny as well. I love to joke and laugh and play around, which also means people love to joke around with me. Every *Halloween*, I think of the tenth grade, when a group of guys heard me talking about hating Michael Meyers from the movie series Halloween. After hearing this, the guys decided to play a joke on me that Halloween with the infamous white Michael Myers mask on. Thirteen guys surrounded my very small ranch home and were at every window. My sister was at the kitchen sink, looked out, and just about peed herself when she saw one of them. When we went outside (just like no one should do if they are truly scared . . .), we saw the guys and the delivery van (from one of their dad's restaurants) and heard the theme music playing from the loudspeaker. *Whose dad has a delivery van with a speaker on top?* Only in a small town . . . The imprint here is, "I hate Halloween movies and scary characters."

One very precious and sweet imprint is a memory of a time when I was in fifth or sixth grade when a new family joined our church. They had a daughter my age who was also clubfooted, and the amazing thing was that her small foot and big foot were the opposite of mine. So, where my left foot is smaller and my right foot is bigger, her left foot is bigger and her right foot is smaller.

Once we met and got to know one another, we figured out we could swap shoes. Since our feet were the same sizes but for the opposite feet, we would swap shoes to give one another the sizes we needed. How awesome is this? It is one of the many reasons I know God always provides and gives us the desires of our hearts if we delight in Him. Only a great, amazing creator could use our physical brokenness to bless another. God knew we'd both have different-sized feet and struggles as a result, but He introduced us to each other.

When you begin to think back, there are many good

Patent Leather—Evaluating the Imprints Formed in Childhood

and bad imprints in your past. Consider how they have shaped you, triggered you, and in some ways, made you who you are today. I could share memories all day about how these imprints have impacted my life, but I will share one more imprint for now that I pray will give you hope.

> *Take delight in the LORD, and he will*
> *give you the desires of your heart.*
> Psalm 37:4, NIV

This memory alone imprinted in me the love of God who cares about me enough to help me, even in a first-world problem of being able to wear shoes I wanted; although, I may not have needed them. Today, when I think of this verse, obviously it is not, nor should it be, about material desires, but it still amazes me that God knew my heart as a little girl and delighted in me to give me shoes that fit. God so delights in you too, and He desires for you to hold on to positive imprints in your life and allow Him to take back patents on any negative ones.

Taking Back What the Devil Stole From Me: Processing Memories that Led to Imprints

There is an old worship song from the 90s that I love titled "Enemy's Camp". The lyrics describe going back to the devil and getting back what he stole from you. If the enemy stole anything from you, by allowing a negative imprint to settle in your mind, I have good news: You can take it back! Processing memories that lead to your imprints is the first step. Earlier, I mentioned the devil using our imprints and wanting to take control of them or put patents on them. By processing old memories, you begin to explore the thoughts, feelings, and associations of imprints of your life. You can take back the patents the devil has tried to place on you.

Imprints from memories such as *I'm fat, I'm unworthy*, or *I'm a failure* can be reprocessed by thinking back and reflecting on the memories in different ways. Many people are terrified to do this because they think they are safer burying past hurts, and that these memories do not impact them if they stay hidden. Others believe these memories are too painful to think about, let alone talk about. But they have impacted us, regardless of whether we think they have or not. If you want to take back the patent from the enemy, you have to think about where your low self-esteem comes from, your fear of Halloween, and where your embarrassment about X, Y, or Z comes from.

I've had clients tell me they felt like a physical weight was lifted off of their chest when they shared and processed painful memories. I always let them know what an honor and privilege it is to hear their stories, and how proud I am of them for sharing. I've been there and am still there; I know it is hard, but it is worth it!

How to Take Back the Patents the Devil Has on Your Imprints: Reprocessing

Reprocessing is the process of looking at old memories with a new lens. I've never worn glasses, but my oldest son wears them. I am intrigued by watching his doctor check his eyesight each year. When she assesses him, she always makes him try with his old prescription strength, then she knows by his response if he needs a stronger or weaker prescription.

In a way, you have to view things through your normal lens, first, and process imprints *before* you can try on a new lens or perspective. Have you ever had your eyes dilated and fitted for a new pair of eyeglasses? I haven't, but my son has. It impacts him for several hours afterward.

Patent Leather—Evaluating the Imprints Formed in Childhood

Learning to see past negative imprints through a new positive lens is challenging and can take some time to get used to, just like a new pair of glasses. I recommend you seek a godly, trained, and licensed counselor/therapist who can help you do so safely. You may even want to ask for a trauma-informed therapist if you have a lot of trauma, such as sexual, physical, spiritual, or emotional abuse. After that first session with a professional, expect your emotional eyes to hurt, just as my son's do after his eyes have been dilated. It takes him a while to get used to the light again. As you try to look at imprints and reprocess them to see how they can make you a stronger or better person, it may be very painful and seem impossible at times. However, with God, all things are possible, and if you are patient with the process, you can experience the miracle God is doing by taking back patents and turning negative imprints into positive ones!

When I looked back at my sexual abuse and thought that the person who tried to abuse me was most likely abused at some point in his life, I didn't want to have any sympathy for him, at first. He was 100% wrong, and there was NO excuse for what he did, but I've also counseled enough people now to know that sexual abuse is typically a cyclical thing. Unless the person abused goes through many different avenues to avoid becoming an abuser, this is often what happens. I've never met an abuser who wasn't abused in his or her past . . . I tread lightly because I know it is painful to go here. When I reprocessed this memory, I asked God to show me how He was with me and how He rescued me. I was also reminded that all humans are broken, as was the abuser in this case. Then, I asked God to help me forgive the person who hurt me. I focused my mind on positive things when this memory came up.

Again, I don't recommend reprocessing trauma alone. You may even want to consider seeing a professional who does Eye Movement Desensitization and Reprocessing (EMDR).

I CAN DO ANYTHING IN THE RIGHT PAIR OF SHOES

This is a psychotherapy for trauma resolution that enables people to heal from the symptoms and emotional distress that are the result of disturbing life experiences.[8]

There are additional ways to reprocess painful memories. Another method is to evaluate how you are a stronger or better person as a result of what has happened to you. I can say that I am very protective over my children and cautious of things that can happen with family and friends. I have prepared my children, family, and friends by talking to them at length about sexual abuse, appropriate touches, etc. Reprocessing in this way has helped me prepare my children to ask for help, fight back, and stand up for others.

God has never wasted my pain. I regularly meet with survivors of sexual abuse, and when I disclose a little of my story, it immediately builds trust. In this way, I have seen God use my story to help others. This is one way I believe we overcome by the word of our testimony as stated in Revelation 12:11. God didn't intend for sexual abuse to ever happen, but He will not waste the pain in a broken world.

I truly despise when people say, "Everything happens for a reason." This implies that everything that happens to us is ultimately good. This is false. I cannot say to a victim of sexual abuse, "Everything happens for a reason." No. The fact of the matter is, bad things happen because we live in a broken and fallen world. However, I can say God has made a way through His Son Jesus for us to be reconciled to Him again. He will redeem us and never waste any pain we have from living in a broken world.

Processing and reprocessing imprints in your life is one way you can put on the shoes of peace and fight against the attacks of the enemy when he tries to bring up past hurts and traumas as a way of stealing your peace. When the enemy tries to attack, put on the shoes of peace by dealing with your past trauma, reminding yourself of the goodness of God who saw you through the painful experiences, and considering how you are becoming a new creation in Christ.

Do not allow the enemy to hold the patent to your hurt. Claim it and process it, so you can allow God to heal you and restore and make beautiful things out of the ashes of your pain. Just like my dad would shine my patent leather shoes and take off all the scuffs every Sunday, let God take your pain and make you shine for Him.

Affirm Yourself Daily by Using "I can" or "I will" Statements

- I can be wise, stand up to a bully, forgive someone, speak the truth in love, etc.
- I will recognize that my parents likely did the best they could, and their inadequacies were not about me.
- I will be responsible for my own feelings and actions, stop looking to others for acceptance, learn to mirror admirable qualities, and practice mindfulness.

Meditate on Scripture:

I will restore to you the years that the swarming locust has eaten, the hopper, the destroyer, and the cutter, my great army, which I sent among you.
Joel 2:25, ESV

Instead of your shame, there shall be a double portion; instead of dishonor they shall rejoice in their lot; therefore in their land they shall possess a double portion; they shall have everlasting joy.
Isaiah 61:7, ESV

I CAN DO ANYTHING IN THE RIGHT PAIR OF SHOES

The thief comes only to steal, kill and destroy. I came that they may have life and have it abundantly.
John 10:10, ESV

The Lord will rescue me from every evil deed and bring me safely into his heavenly kingdom. To him be the glory forever and ever. Amen.
2 Timothy 4:18, NIV

No weapon that is fashioned against you shall succeed, and you shall confute every tongue that rises against you in judgment. This is the heritage of the servants of the Lord and their vindication from me, declares the Lord.
Isaiah 54:17, NIV

And the Lord restored the fortunes of Job when he had prayed for his friends. And the Lord gave Job twice as much as he had before.
Job 42:10, ESV

Behold, all who are incensed against you shall be put to shame and confounded; those who strive against you shall be as nothing and shall perish.
Isaiah 41:11, ESV

I will give you the keys of the kingdom of heaven, and whatever you bind on earth shall be bound in heaven, and whatever you loose on earth shall be loosed in heaven.
Matthew 16:19, NIV

And Zacchaeus stood and said to the Lord, "Behold, Lord, the half of my goods I give to the poor. And if I have defrauded anyone of anything, I restore it fourfold."
Luke 19:8, NIV

Patent Leather—Evaluating the Imprints Formed in Childhood

Return to your stronghold, O prisoners of hope; today I declare that I will restore to you double.
Zechariah 9:12, NIV

Do not say, "I will repay evil;" wait for the Lord, and he will deliver you.
Proverbs 20:22, NIV

When the righteous cry for help, the Lord hears and delivers them out of all their troubles.
Psalm 34:17, NIV

Your right hand, O Lord, glorious in power, your right hand, O Lord, shatters the enemy.
Exodus 15:6, NIV

Through you we push down our foes; through your name we tread down those who rise against us.
Psalm 44:5, ESV

He said, "The Lord is my rock and my fortress and my deliverer.
2 Samuel 22:2, ESV

Write/Journal:

Write out the imprints you've uncovered in your life. Consider writing them out in increments of five to ten years, based on good and bad experiences in your life. Ask yourself, "What events or experiences do I remember as significant between ages X-X?" Next to these notations, answer the question: Who was one person(s) who was helpful to me during this time?

I CAN DO ANYTHING IN THE RIGHT PAIR OF SHOES

Examples:

-Zero-five years: I was born with clubbed feet. My godparents supported my parents as if they were family.

-Six-ten years: I changed schools, and my mom had a baby. My mom's friend took us to school when my mom couldn't.

-Keep going in five-year increments up to your current age.

Next, write out how some of the bad things in your life have been used for your good or others' benefit. You are now protective, vigilant, and an advocate for the orphans. You take your role as a godparent seriously, etc.

I can walk in peace by not allowing the negative imprints from my childhood to define the rest of my life.

PART TWO

Fighting the Enemy with Peace in the Present

"Cinderella proves that a new pair of shoes can change your life."
— Noortje de Bijl, Designer[9]

FOUR

The Cinderella Squeeze— Good vs. Bad Comparison

When I was in fourth grade, Sam & Libby flats, with a big bow on them, in a variety of colors, were all the rage. I wanted a pair like everyone else. The problem was, my feet were not like everyone else. My feet were two very different sizes! My parents couldn't buy me one pair of shoes to fit both of my feet, and it was too expensive to buy two pairs. Currently, my feet are sizes six and eight. In case math isn't your thing, that is a *two-size difference!* At times, it feels like I should be a circus freak as I compare myself to others with the same-sized feet.

Thomas Mussweiler, a professor of organizational behavior, describes comparison this way: "It's one of the most basic ways we develop an understanding of who we are, what we're good at, and what we're not so good at. Most of the time, we make this calculation in a split second in the background, and we don't even realize it. But when we dwell on the highlights of other people's lives, it can quickly become toxic. We're wired for connection and belonging, but if we constantly compare ourselves to others, we're putting our happiness, confidence, and mental health at risk."[10]

Comparison is inevitable, but it is also dangerous. Just

I CAN DO ANYTHING IN THE RIGHT PAIR OF SHOES

like dynamite can be devastating unless used for good reasons, comparison can also be detrimental if used in the wrong ways. It is normal and okay to admire others and to be positively influenced by others at times. It wasn't a bad thing that I wanted a pair of Sam & Libby shoes. It would have been bad, though, if I'd thought I wasn't as good as others who had these shoes or if I let a style of shoe or status associated with those shoes define me. Do you remember allowing a style, or lack of one, to define you in the past?

I'm sure, in the fourth grade, I thought the shoes were cute, and at some level, I wanted to be like the other girls who had them. My grandmother also felt for me and wanted me to have those shoes to make me happy. She didn't want me to feel like I was a kid known for having disabled feet. She hated that I compared myself to other kids who could wear any shoes, and she understood how I felt, but she considered me to be special. She decided to write letters to the corporation that sold those shoes and others.

My grandmother wasn't advocating for me because she thought I needed them to be as good as everyone else. She was showing love for her granddaughter. Although she had an eighth-grade education, her letter was so convincing that Belk Corporation wrote her back, allowing my family to receive a discount every time I needed to buy more than one pair of shoes. I can assure you that if she thought the shoes were about me comparing myself to others in a negative way, she wouldn't have fought for me.

I share this story to alleviate the frustration of feeling like you can't stop something that often seems automatic. If we had a quarter for every time we compared ourselves with others, we'd be well on our way to being able to fund our kids' college without a 529 savings plan, paying for very nice retirement living, funding a school in Africa; you name it! Comparison feels automatic at times, but while it seems like something

The Cinderella Squeeze—Good vs. Bad Comparison

in your personal diet, you must give up. It needs to be used with caution and in moderation, much like chocolate in my daily diet.

The enemy loves to fight us each day, so we must put on our shoes of peace by understanding how he negatively uses comparison to keep us defeated. He uses comparison in negative ways to distort our view of who we are supposed to be as unique creations of God.

Consider the narrative of the story of Cinderella. Rewrite the story in your mind as if the stepsister had found the glass slipper and was excited to return it to her sister instead of trying to squeeze herself into it. Squeezing into being something or someone we are not is painful and can cause a great deal of harm. Can you imagine the blisters and sores the stepsisters experienced trying to be Cinderella? At times, comparison can be a great motivator for us to take action in positive directions, but if we allow comparison to lead us down paths of wanting to be in someone's shoes or have them as our own, it's ugly.

Another struggle with comparison is when we perceive others are comparing themselves to us. For some reason, we can feel threatened when others seem to be comparing themselves to us. Most of the time, we don't want to be compared to others, whether we are the ones doing it or not. We almost feel like, if they compare, they must want what we have. However, this may not always be the case. They may want to try something they like because it is admirable. Do you allow others to be inspired by you?

During the summer of 2001, I was in the World Trade Center before the tragic events of 9/11. There was this amazing underground mall of sorts, and I was shopping in the J. Crew store. As a lover of shoes, I tried on a pair I liked and walked over to show my friends. When I walked back to where I'd left my shoes they weren't there. I knew I hadn't walked into the store barefoot, so I looked around for them.

Eventually, I noticed a lady trying on my shoes as if they were for sale. Without thinking before reacting, I said, "Hey those are MY shoes," in a way that may have scared her a bit. My friends looked up to see what was wrong and started laughing. They joked with me about this incident years later because it is funny, in hindsight. I wish I had noticed the humor in the moment and said to the lady instead, "Well, hello; those shoes look amazing on you, but they are not actually for sale."

Oftentimes, we view the idea of comparison negatively. Sure; comparison is often crafted as a weapon of the enemy when it comes to walking in peace each day. The enemy's tactic of tempting us to seek resemblance with others can lead to anxious thoughts, overspending, and even depression. But I believe we can use comparison positively and learn to stop using it as a careless tool. While we can't be prepared with the feet of peace if we are constantly pointing out what we lack, we can learn how comparison can be used healthily.

What God's Word Says about Peace and Comparison

Paul, an apostle of Jesus and arguably the greatest missionary who ever lived, wrote this to a church he loved in Rome:

It is written: "As surely as I live," says the Lord, "every knee will bow before me; every tongue will acknowledge God." So then, each of us will give an account of ourselves to God. Therefore let us stop passing judgment on one another. Instead, make up your mind not to put any stumbling block or obstacle in the way of a brother or sister. I am convinced, being fully persuaded in the Lord Jesus, that nothing is unclean

The Cinderella Squeeze—Good vs. Bad Comparison

in itself. But if anyone regards something as unclean, then for that person it is unclean. If your brother or sister is distressed because of what you eat, you are no longer acting in love. Do not by your eating destroy someone for whom Christ died. Therefore do not let what you know is good be spoken of as evil. For the kingdom of God is not a matter of eating and drinking, but of righteousness, peace and joy in the Holy Spirit, because anyone who serves Christ in this way is pleasing to God and receives human approval. Let us therefore make every effort to do what leads to peace and to mutual edification.
Romans 14:11–19, ESV

Paul encourages believers by teaching them how to interact with one another. He discusses, in this passage, the truth that we will all, individually, give an account of our lives. Then, he goes on to address the behaviors of others and how they impact one another. Paul concludes by stating that the kingdom of God isn't about any activity other than righteousness, peace, and joy in the Holy Spirit, which pleases God. He says to quit worrying about human approval, then instructs them to do everything that leads to peace and mutual edification. When you are edifying or uplifting someone else, and that person does this in return, this can lead you both to a more peaceful walk in life.

I love this passage of Scripture because I see how God wants us to stop comparing ourselves to one another negatively and instead "make every effort to do what leads to peace and to mutual edification" (v. 19). I have to believe this means the two (peace and mutual edification) go hand in hand. In other words, when we build one another up, we are also doing things that lead to peace! What can you do today to build someone up in a way that leads to peace?

I CAN DO ANYTHING IN THE RIGHT PAIR OF SHOES

Here are a few other verses to meditate on if you struggle with comparison:

You shall not covet your neighbor's house; you shall not covet your neighbor's wife, or his male servant, or his female servant, or his ox, or his donkey, or anything that is your neighbor's.
Exodus 20:7, ESV

Do you struggle with coveting or desiring what someone else has? Do you go on social media to see what others have, what they are doing, or what they are wearing? Let's consider why God commands us not to covet. Could it be that it hurts us? Maybe it even potentially kills our happiness and contentment?

Love is patient, love is kind. It does not envy, it does not boast, it is not proud. It does not dishonor others, it is not self-seeking, it is not easily angered, it keeps no record of wrongs. Love does not delight in evil but rejoices with the truth. It always protects, always trusts, always hopes, always perseveres.
1 Corinthians 13:4–8, ESV

This passage describes love, indicating that love doesn't envy. Therefore, who or what are we not loving if we are envying? Can we truly love those around us if we are consumed with envy?

But if you harbor bitter envy and selfish ambition in your hearts, do not boast about it or deny the truth. Such "wisdom" does not come down from heaven but is earthly, unspiritual, demonic. For where you have envy and selfish ambition, there you find disorder

The Cinderella Squeeze—Good vs. Bad Comparison

and every evil practice.
James 3:14–16, ESV

James just gave us what I call a throat punch. He hit us with truth but from a heart of love. He knew that if we harbor bitter envy and selfishness in our hearts, it would ultimately destroy us. He even called it demonic and evil. I don't know about you, but I do not want Satan parking his boat anywhere near my harbor, which is my heart/mind/soul/emotions.

For it is by grace you have been saved, through faith—and this is not from yourselves, it is the gift of God— not by works, so that no one can boast. For we are God's handiwork, created in Christ Jesus to do good works, which God prepared in advance for us to do.
Ephesians 2:8–10, ESV

According to God's Word, we cannot boast about anything. We should never seek to boast or compare ourselves to others! We are all God's molded creations, here to do the good works He alone calls us to do. This should be on a bookmark, sticky note, or your daily calendar, reminding you not to boast but to thank God for His gift of grace. Satan loves to make us forget this. It is nice to receive praise for good work, but we have to lay that praise at the feet of Jesus daily or it could destroy us by allowing self-aggrandizement to take root. Do you regularly lay praise you've received at the feet of Jesus?

A dispute also arose among them, as to which of them was to be regarded as the greatest. And he said to them, "The kings of the Gentiles exercise lordship over them, and those in authority over them are called benefactors. But not so with you. Rather, let the greatest among you become as the youngest, and the leader as one who

I CAN DO ANYTHING IN THE RIGHT PAIR OF SHOES

serves. For who is the greater, one who reclines at table or one who serves? Is it not the one who reclines at table? But I am among you as the one who serves."
Luke 22:24–27, ESV

Maybe you haven't done this as openly as the disciples, or maybe you have, but we've all probably done it in our hearts and minds. We want to talk about who does more at church, who does more for our aging parents, who does more work in the office, who does more work at home. The list could go on. I've done it and still struggle, at times, but thankfully, God reminds us we are called to serve. One thing I've learned is that when you do all to serve the Lord and not yourself or others, it brings so much more joy into your life. Who doesn't need more joy? Be careful not to make this about comparing yourself in terms of you serving more than someone else. The focus is to do what God has called you to—serve, and do so gladly!

Not that we dare to classify or compare ourselves with some of those who are commending themselves. But when they measure themselves by one another and compare themselves with one another, they are without understanding.
2 Corinthians 10:12, ESV

This passage suggests that people who compare themselves with others, to commend themselves, are without understanding. God doesn't compare us to others. He will judge us according to the gifts He has given us, not how we measure up compared to others. Therefore, why do we find ourselves comparing ourselves to others on social media, at work, or wherever? Instead, let's find reasons to improve where we can and be content when we need to be, with how God made us. You will feel much more peace in your life when you are thankful for the shoes you have and stop desiring the shoes of another.

Practical Steps to Reframe Comparison

To make sure you use comparison wisely, consider measuring it in terms of the following feelings: envy, jealousy, strife, covetousness, and justice. First, let's define these terms.

Envy is a feeling of discontentment concerning the advantages or success of others.

Jealousy is mental uneasiness from suspicion or fear of rivalry.

Strife is vigorous or bitter discord.

Covetousness is an eager or excessive desire to have what someone else has.

Justice is the idea of equitableness. This can cause stress in the area of comparison if you are keeping score and wanting everything in life to be equal when it is not entirely possible in a broken world.

We can walk in peace and put on the readiness of the gospel by guarding ourselves from the lies of the enemy who tempts us to compare us to others. One way we can fight the enemy is by reframing the sins (envy, jealousy, strife, covetousness, unhealthy focus on justice) that come along with comparison. Ask yourself these questions:

- Envy: *When I am tempted to compare, do I feel discontent as I see the success of others? Am I happy for them?*

- Jealousy: *Do I see a social media post from someone in my past and feel terrible because they seem to be doing better than I am in some area?*
- Strife: *Do I feel bitter when I see someone has succeeded in an area where I am struggling?*
- Covetousness: *Do I desire to have what someone else has?*
- Justice: *Am I constantly saying something isn't fair?*

Reframe by stating the following phrases in response to negative comparison:

- Life isn't fair, fair isn't always equal, and comparisons are never fair.
- Social media is an illusion.
- Comparison can harm your relationships by turning friends into enemies.
- There is beauty in the difference.
- Comparison is not God's design. We are unique.
- God can use my struggle to bless others.
- God never wastes my pain.

The Beatitudes of Healthy Comparison

Blessed are the peacemakers, for they shall be called sons of God.
Matthew 5:9, NIV

Years ago, my cousin's husband joked with her and me about not affording Louis Vuitton (I had to look up the spelling of that brand name). It was during a time when friends were having parties selling knock-off, famous-brand purses.

The Cinderella Squeeze—Good vs. Bad Comparison

I'm not even sure if it is legal. Still, an officer never showed up to any party I attended . . . Nonetheless, my cousin's husband asked, after one of the parties (in a very southern accent), "Did you buy one of those *Larry* Vuitton purses?" Jokingly, he gave the brand a knock-off name! I'm not sure he was trying to be a peacemaker by saying this. However, laughter can be a great way to combat negative comparisons and a great way to choose to walk in peace. We still laugh about our *Larry* Vuitton purses.

It is 100% okay to enjoy name brands and knock-off brands, but let's make sure our comparisons are used in ways that bring peace. Put on the shoes of peace today by appreciating who God made you. Be thankful for the differences of others, and resist the devil by reframing negative comparisons. Finally, plant your feet firmly in the word of God by meditating on His truths to help you stop the attacks of negative comparison by the enemy.

Ways to combat comparison:
1. Be thankful, and practice gratitude.
2. Be content.
3. Be aware that social media is only the "highlight reel."
4. Be strong in who you are and who God created you to be.
5. Be happy for others.
6. Be a self-competitor.
7. Be someone who is social offline, not just online. Set boundaries for social media.

Good times to compare:
- When there is something to learn.
- To be inspired to do good or improve in an area.
- To gain a positive perspective.

I CAN DO ANYTHING IN THE RIGHT PAIR OF SHOES

- When you can remain in your lane, you can safely admire someone else.
- Show the possibility of what could be or hope for the future.
- Positive competition for notable causes.
- Past self: I'm not who I once was.

Meditate on these verses, if you struggle with comparison:

But the fruit of the Spirit is love, joy, peace, forbearance, kindness, goodness, faithfulness, gentleness and self-control. Against such things there is no law. Those who belong to Christ Jesus have crucified the flesh with its passions and desires. Since we live by the Spirit, let us keep in step with the Spirit.
Galatians 5:22–25, ESV

For am I now seeking the approval of man, or of God? Or am I trying to please man? If I were still trying to please man, I would not be a servant of Christ.
Galatians 1:10, ESV

For if anyone thinks he is something, when he is nothing, he deceives himself. But let each one test his own work, and then his reason to boast will be in himself alone and not in his neighbor. For each will have to bear his own load.
Galatians 6:3–5, ESV

I can walk in peace by allowing others to inspire me and not give in to comparing myself with others in negative ways.

FIVE

Loafers — Letting Go of Comforts

Always, in all circumstances, wear comfortable shoes.
You never know when you may have to run for your life.
— Callie Kouri, television screenwriter[11]

Do you know what "old lady shoes" are? My grandmother used to wear Easy Spirit shoes. She had them in multiple colors and claimed they were super comfortable. My grandmother also had struggles with her feet and legs. She was born with a bone disorder and had severe leg and foot problems that caused pain throughout her life. She spent most of the first two years of her life in the hospital because of her bone disease.

To say I get my strong will from her is likely very true! She sought out the comfort of shoes in her older age due to her need to walk with extra support. Despite her comfortable shoes, she would have never described her life as comfortable. She struggled, she worked hard, she prayed hard, and she also laughed hard . . . at least with me. Grandma had peace in her life, but she did not have daily comfort.

For some reason, many people believe comfort leads to peace. I disagree.

The Comfort Zone: What It Is, and Why People Want to Stay There

Many people in developed nations have taken comfort way too far. Have you ever noticed how many mattress stores there are or commercials for pillows? I've even recently heard that some cars have massage chairs in them. We are blessed to have so many physical, financial, and environmental comforts. We are so used to certain things like running water, that honestly, I think it is out of fear we seek to remain in our comfort zones.

What is the comfort zone anyway, and why do so many seek to stay in it?

Comfort-seeking can be defined as the pursuit of physical, mental, and social ease. The phrase "comfort zone" was coined by management thinker Judith Bardwick, in her 1991 work, *Danger in the Comfort Zone*. She notes: "The comfort zone is a behavioral state within which a person operates in an anxiety-neutral condition, using a limited set of behaviors to deliver a steady level of performance, usually without a sense of risk."[12]

This sounds nice and fancy; however, consider how difficult it is to go through life trying to stay in this place. Furthermore, is "anxiety-neutral" even possible in a fallen and broken world?

Anxiety has gotten a bad reputation. Some anxiety is normal and can help you prepare for a challenging moment. If you never had a little anxiety about a test, you'd never study. If you never had a little anxiety about driving, you might just close your eyes and hit the road. The key to managing anxious thoughts and moments of anxiety is not overcorrecting by having too much anxiety or seeking to stay in the "anxiety-neutral zone." God gave us life to live, so we should live it by trying new things, pushing ourselves at times, and yes, even allowing ourselves to be uncomfortable. When was the last time you allowed yourself to feel discomfort?

Here is a way to gauge your comfort in different areas:

Physically:

Have you challenged yourself physically, lately? This morning, I ran six miles, not because I just love it, but because I know physical fitness and pushing my body is healthy, at times. Many of us need to evaluate how we stay within our physical comfort zones and contemplate how we can challenge ourselves. Maybe it's to eat healthily. In our world of fast food and convenience, it can be very comfortable to eat what is there instead of seeking a healthy lifestyle. Consider, for a moment, all of the times today you went for an easy, convenient, or comfortable food instead of a healthy choice.

Another area of a physical challenge is taking time to rest. Some people do not know how to prioritize sleep and rest, and, on the other hand, some put too much priority on it. For example, I know some who do not prioritize sleep and overwork constantly, staying in a state of stress. I also know people who want to sleep all weekend and never hang out with friends or do other things. This can negatively impact their relationships.

Spiritually:

Have you allowed God to challenge you spiritually? Do you read God's Word daily, so you can be refined by Him? Have you spent time with God's children lately, so you can be challenged interpersonally? I went with a friend on my run this morning, and as we vented and talked about life, she challenged me to think about a tough situation in a different way. She encouraged me to see the Lord could be using my current frustration to teach me something or possibly protect me from something. At church yesterday, I was convicted to seek Jesus more than I seek miracles. Seeking Jesus helps me to truly focus on being thankful, regardless of whether a miracle happens in my life or not. Allowing myself to be challenged and convicted, spiritually, by a friend, on a run, or through a sermon, helps me to grow.

One way I challenge myself daily is by reading the Proverb correlating with the number of the day (i.e. If today is the 5th, I will read Proverbs 5, and so on.). Another way to push yourself out of your spiritual comfort zone is through fasting. When was the last time you fasted? Fasting can bring you so much closer to God.

Finally, when was the last time you were "still" before and with the Lord? Talk about being out of your comfort zone. Some cannot imagine sitting in silence these days. We have noise from all angles (technology, earbuds, social media, etc . . .). Satan does not want you to realize when you've grown comfortable in your spiritual walk, because when we are comfortable, we are, in essence, ineffective for the kingdom. Reflecting on your spiritual walk regularly, and putting ongoing practices in place to challenge yourself spiritually, can help you walk in peace and guard against complacency.

Intellectually:

Have you pushed your intellect lately? There is the belief that Alzheimer's can be prevented, or at least pushed off, longer by doing things such as puzzles, word searches, brain teasers, and reading. Your mind needs to be pushed. When was the last time you learned a new skill, a new language, or tried a new food? Have you read or listened to a good book lately?

Getting out of your comfort zone to read, learn, do a puzzle, or have a deep conversation with someone, to challenge yourself intellectually, can have benefits beyond preventing dementia. Consider, for a moment, how your life could change if you spoke another language, for example. Sure, it might be challenging to learn another language, but if you did, you could open yourself up to a whole new people group! At the very least, you could understand what someone who speaks a different language is saying if they are providing a service to you, such as at the nail salon.

Socially:

When was the last time you challenged yourself socially? Have you made a new friend lately? Have you met someone who was from a different ethnicity, culture, or religion? Challenging yourself socially is something Jesus modeled for us. He often engaged with Samaritans and tax collectors—people from all walks of life. Why do we not do the same?

I love the idea of Mark Twain that the cure for prejudice is travel. He said, "Travel is fatal to prejudice, bigotry, and narrow-mindedness, and many of our people need it sorely on these accounts. Broad, wholesome, charitable views of men and things cannot be acquired by vegetating in one little corner of the earth all one's lifetime."[13] This seems to suggest Mark Twain believed in the value of learning from others. When was the last time you helped someone who was in need? I drove a hitchhiker home the other day. I realize this can be very dangerous, but I prayed and felt like God wanted me to take this sweet lady home from the grocery store. I did, and you know what; I feel as if I were more blessed than she was. The opportunity had come at the end of a heartbreaking week. God used the chance to bless this lady in a very small way to remind me that we, "Overcome evil by doing good" (Romans 12:21, ESV). It brought me so much peace after a long week.

Emotionally:

When was the last time you challenged yourself emotionally? Have you allowed yourself to think back on painful things in the past, seeking to process and reprocess them effectively? Have you allowed yourself to cry lately? Conversely, have you allowed yourself to laugh? What about considering the emotions of others? Have you allowed others to be vulnerable around you?

Listen; although I'm a counselor, at times, I don't want to talk about things and deal with my emotions. However, when I challenge myself and put in the work to deal with my emotions surrounding different things in my life, growth happens. It also helps me to understand how hard talking to a stranger can be when a client comes into my office for the first time.

Financially:

This may seem like an odd area to consider, but undoubtedly, it is an important one to note. Your comfort zone here can also be extreme on one end or another. You may need to learn to be uncomfortable and save some money or pay off some credit cards, or you may need to spend a little and enjoy life some more. Comfort, in this category, can be defined in terms of extremes on either end. You can't possibly walk in peace by spending every dime you have nor can you walk in peace if you are too scared to spend anything.

Trying New Things/Adventures:

This is an area people think of most often when it comes to comfort zones. People think getting out of your comfort zone means jumping out of an airplane, which isn't necessarily true; though, it was for me. I went skydiving for my fortieth birthday. I'm an adventurous person by nature, but it still wasn't a comfortable thing for me to do. It did feel great to do something scary and to survive it. For others, it might be public speaking. For one of my podcast episodes, I interviewed my skydiving instructor. He told me and my co-host/friend,

Candice, he was so nervous to be on our podcast. Can you believe that? A guy who jumps out of planes daily for a living was scared to be interviewed for a small-town girl podcast. I share the story to help you see that stepping out of your comfort zone can be different for everyone. However, you must try new things. Try new adventures, or you will miss out on so much of the wonder of the world and God. You will struggle to walk in peace because, frankly, you won't be walking at all.

Problems with Comfort

Some people think it is ridiculous to wear uncomfortable shoes, but who hasn't had to break into an awesome pair of shoes? We break them in, the shoes become super comfortable, then they fall apart, and we have to start all over again. Isn't life like this sometimes? We begin new friendships, jobs, churches, have kids, etc. Sometimes these things become comfortable, and sometimes they don't, but it is an ongoing process. If we never try to break into something new, we will miss out on some great things, experiences, and most importantly people.

When we seek comfort for ourselves, it often causes the suffering of others. If we stay in our comfort zone physically, spiritually, intellectually, financially, emotionally, or socially, we often do it without thinking about how it impacts others. As a mother, if I never try new things, imagine the number of opportunities my kids may miss out on. If I hoard all of my money and never give, there may be some people who won't eat. If I never try to make new friends, someone may not be blessed by friendship. Do you see it? Every action or inaction has consequences. If you seek to stay in your comfort zone, don't think for one second that it will not impact others. It will!

The list could go on, but another problem with com-

I CAN DO ANYTHING IN THE RIGHT PAIR OF SHOES

fort is that for those of us who are followers of Jesus, He did not come to make us comfortable; He came to set us free. The enemy often lies and tries to pervert the truth by suggesting that we should seek to stay in our comfort zone, at all costs. Satan, our true enemy, doesn't want us to be free!

In Galatians 5:1, Paul said, "It was for freedom that Christ set us free; therefore keep standing firm and do not be subject again to a yoke of slavery." "Yoke" may sound like a weird word to those of us born in the twentieth or twenty-first century, but it was a Biblical term used to describe a tool used to tie oxen together. The yoke was a wooden contraption that fastened two animals together to a plow, so the animals could pull the load together. God used the term yoke in multiple ways in Scripture (sixty times) to discuss slavery, service, position, or influence in relationships.

Jesus wants us to be free from the yoke of comfort. He wants us to be free to be who and what He created us to be. Jesus didn't come to make us comfortable; He came to set us free, and in turn, give us a peace we can put on and walk in daily. Don't be enslaved to comfort. Don't be yoked to it. Allow Jesus to set you free.

Activity: Moving From the Comfort Zone to the Growth Zone

Review the chart below.[14]

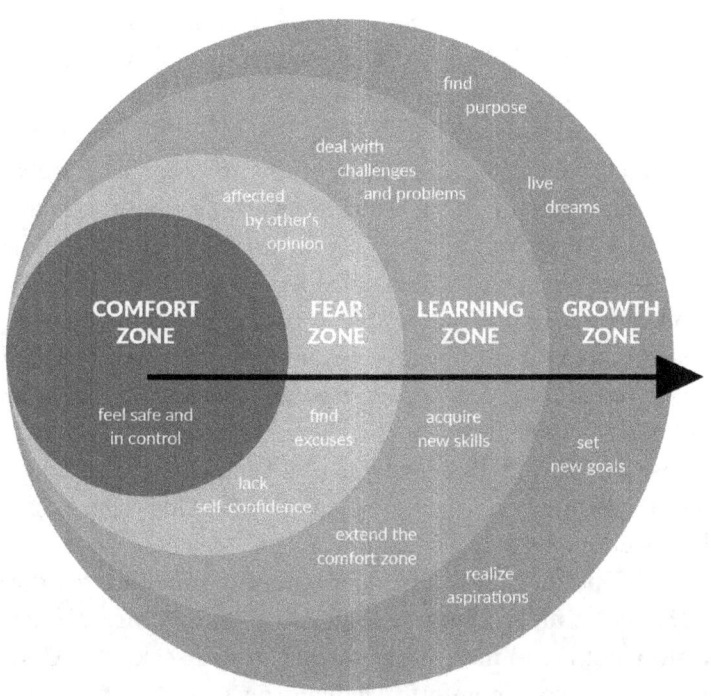

Now, think of your comforts and fears, and write them out.

Next, draw your own chart.

Then, write your comforts in the chart, followed by your fears.

Next, write what you need or want to learn.

Finally, write out how you plan to move into the growth zone.

I CAN DO ANYTHING IN THE RIGHT PAIR OF SHOES

I'll never forget the penny loafers my godfather used to wear when he and my godmother would come to see me and my sisters at one of our piano recitals or church. Yes, he, literally, put a penny in them, which, as a kid, I thought was super cool. The word *loafer* may sound comfortable to you, but to me, it sounds ineffective. Strolling along in life as comfortably as possible may feel good at the moment, but it is ineffective at bringing peace into your life long-term.

Remember, getting outside of our comfort zone can be *life-changing*. Letting go of comforts involves embracing challenges and allowing discomfort to grow spiritually, mentally, and physically. Walking in peace is not the same as walking in comfort. Your brain often considers what is comfortable as good and what is uncomfortable as bad, which is very dangerous and often misleading. Your brain may say, stay in bed if it is comfortable, or eat the entire cake because it'll make you feel better momentarily. Feelings can be misleading. So don't choose to always follow feelings sent from your brain. Choosing to walk in peace is about having faith in God regardless of the uncertainty of your situation.

The fact that Jesus set us free is much better than if He had simply come to make us comfortable. We have to stop looking to the world for comfort and seek what God's word says about comfort. Meditate on God's word, if you struggle with staying in a comfort zone. God wants to be our source of comfort.

Use these verses for meditation:

I remain confident of this: I will see the goodness of the LORD in the land of the living. Wait for the LORD; be strong and take heart and wait for the LORD.
Psalm 27:13-14, ESV

Loafers—Letting Go of Comforts

This verse is about someone who is actively choosing to see the goodness of the Lord. Do you actively choose to see good, even when you feel discomfort?

Don't be afraid, for I am with you. Don't be discouraged, for I am your God. I will strengthen you and help you. I will hold you up with my victorious right hand.
Isaiah 41:10, ESV

When you try new things or are challenged, remember God is with you.

Comfort, comfort my people, says your God. Speak tenderly to Jerusalem, and proclaim to her that her hard service has been completed, that her sin has been paid for, that she has received from the LORD's hand double for all her sins. A voice of one calling: "In the wilderness prepare the way for the LORD ; make straight in the desert a highway for our God. Every valley shall be raised up, every mountain and hill made low; the rough ground shall become level, the rugged places a plain. And the glory of the LORD will be revealed, and all people will see it together. For the mouth of the LORD has spoken.
Isaiah 40:1-11, ESV

At times, we are uncomfortable due to the poor choices we have made, so this passage encourages us to find comfort in that God has paid the price for our sins! This should encourage us to keep going in life and keep trying. Our failures do not define us, nor should we be afraid of trying!

Blessed are those who mourn, for they will be comforted.
Matthew 5:4, ESV

I CAN DO ANYTHING IN THE RIGHT PAIR OF SHOES

Paul, an apostle of Christ Jesus by the will of God, and Timothy our brother, To the church of God in Corinth, together with all his holy people throughout Achaia: Grace and peace to you from God our Father and the Lord Jesus Christ. Praise be to the God and Father of our Lord Jesus Christ, the Father of compassion and the God of all comfort, who comforts us in all our troubles, so that we can comfort those in any trouble with the comfort we ourselves receive from God.
2 Corinthians 1:1-4, ESV

Come to me, all you who are weary and burdened, and I will give you rest. Take my yoke upon you and learn from me, for I am gentle and humble in heart, and you will find rest for your souls. For my yoke is easy and my burden is light.
Matthew 11:28-30, ESV

Even though I walk through the darkest valley, I will fear no evil, for you are with me; your rod and your staff, they comfort me.
Psalm 23:4, ESV

In the same way, the Spirit helps us in our weakness. We do not know what we ought to pray for, but the Spirit himself intercedes for us through wordless groans. And he who searches our hearts knows the mind of the Spirit, because the Spirit intercedes for God's people in accordance with the will of God. And we know that in all things God works for the good of those who love him, who have been called according to his purpose.
Romans 8:26-28, ESV

Give me a sign of your goodness, that my enemies may see it and be put to shame, for you, LORD,

Loafers—Letting Go of Comforts

have helped me and comforted me.
Psalm 86:17, NIV

I can walk in peace by letting go of my comforts.

SIX

Shoes as a "Push Present" —Preparing for the Unexpected

"I don't know why my shoes are so popular - I am always surprised and mystified by them."
— Manolo Blahnik, fashion designer[15]

    My husband, *God love him*, is a wonderful gift giver, but when he showed up after I gave birth to our first son with a pair of running shoes, I definitely was not prepared to respond well. My response was more of a tearful, hormonal growl, based on the assumption he wanted me to get back to exercising soon. We prepare for many things in life, but rarely do we plan for the unexpected. Adequately preparing your heart and mind for unexpected things in life must involve spending time daily falling in love with Jesus, the Prince of Peace.

    So, the story goes like this: "Honey, after I give birth and recover, I'd like to try running." I'd always hated it in the past and never thought I could do it, but why not? At the time, my friend worked at a running store that was very popular in our area. Therefore, when my husband heard, "She wants to start running", he thought the perfect gift would be a new pair of running shoes, recommended by my friend. He brought them proudly to the hospital and gave them to me while I was still laid up from giving birth.

    Becoming a mom for the first time is overwhelming,

to say the least. You go from basically being able to control everything inside your body to immediately trying to keep the baby alive. Consequently, in the overwhelmed state I was in, when my husband walked in with running shoes, all I could think he was suggesting was, "Get your fat butt running, so you can get in shape and lose the baby weight as soon as possible." This is, of course, not at all what he was suggesting.

As you can imagine, this added to overwhelming feelings, and the tears started flowing as did my sarcasm. My sweet husband felt horrible. Ladies, let me interject some words of wisdom after almost two decades of marriage and being a marriage counselor; men are not mind-readers. They are not wired like you or me. They do not get hints. Men are practical and mostly left-brained. They are typically not trying to hurt you or upset your emotional well-being. They are simple.

My husband was simply trying to give me a gift. Granted, I had to tell him, as he is not a mind reader, that running shoes are never a great gift to bring to a lady who just gave birth. Needless to say, he came back the next day with a pearl bracelet.

We prepare for many things in life, but rarely do we plan for the unexpected. Preparing for the unexpected is something that can be difficult to do, as it often involves thinking of things that you often don't want to think about. I'm not sure I could have prepared myself for my husband's push present, but preparing myself to love him well and be honest with him was helpful. I do not always do this well. There have been A LOT of trial-and-error moments over the years.

Because I struggled with my feet over the years, I prepare each day with careful consideration for what shoes I wear. Rain boots are obviously for those days when there is a monsoon outside. When I travel, I consider how long I'll be in a pair of shoes, how much walking I'll be doing, etc. The same applies to the shoes of peace in the armor of God. Did you

Shoes as a "Push Present"—Preparing for the Unexpected

know the shoes of peace from the armor of God were designed with defensive and offensive strategies in mind, to combat the attacks of the enemy?

Much like a battle strategy, putting on the shoes of peace, daily and intentionally, can help you prepare for the unexpected things in life. Whether good or bad circumstances come your way on a given day, putting on the shoes of peace is vital. Choosing to *wear* peace, as a part of your armor, will give you the right perspective going into any situation.

Often, the first step in dealing with unexpected things is to think about circumstances beforehand. So, let's think about some unexpected things in life that no one wants to think about, let alone prepare for:

Death

Yes; I went there as the first thing no one wants to talk about. It is often listed as the biggest fear among most people. As you think about this topic, I want you to be broad. Think about the simple things first, such as your car, phone, or computer dying. This is frustrating and often unexpected. How can you prepare for this? As a sixteen-year-old, I didn't expect my car to die on the first day I drove it to school. Okay; to be fair, it ran out of gas because the gas gauge was dead . . . I didn't have AAA at the time, but I was able to laugh at the situation later. Preparing not to sweat the small stuff, in this instance, helped me.

Next, ease into thinking about the more serious subjects where death could or has affected you, such as losing a pet, parent, sibling, friend, or child. Death is often unexpected and tragic. I'm sure my parents didn't plan for the birth of their twin daughters to end in death.

Death always stinks, in one way or another. It causes everything to stop, things to change, issues to be faced. When death happens, it is painful; however, it can be sweet if the person is a believer in Jesus and is going to heaven. This may sound strange, but I often prepare for awkward moments at funerals or wakes by looking for moments of humor. I'll never forget the time my husband was cornered by a family member when my grandmother died, and later, he asked me, "Who was that pothead that cornered me?" He was not prepared for that conversation. Humor is a gift from God; it doesn't change the situation, but it can change your mood. Choosing to laugh instead of getting upset is a way of putting on shoes of peace.

Finding humor during difficult times can be challenging; especially while dealing with loss. I often tell clients I believe death is so hard, because we were created to live forever, and our bodies, minds, and hearts are not designed to deal with death. God even created our bodies to heal themselves on some levels. Death is at the top of the list of things no one wants to prepare for or think about. However, thinking about it, and somewhat preparing your mind for it, can be a way of finding peace with it.

I will say that while I didn't want to think about something happening to me or my husband when my kids were little, or even now, having our will prepared, and knowing they would be taken care of, according to our wishes, gives me peace. Just as knowing my loved ones who have gone before me are in heaven, I have peace knowing I'll see them again.

Accidents

Do you know someone who has been tragically hurt in a freak accident? Most of us, sadly, do. This could include so many different things. One day, at the gym where my family works out, an employee found my husband and told him our son was bleeding. At first, my husband said, "He'll be fine. Tell him to clean up and keep going." Don't judge us. After years of

Shoes as a "Push Present" — Preparing for the Unexpected

having boys, you have to develop this attitude. However, this time, the employee said, "No; you have to come, now." Immediately, he ran to the aid of our son. Our boys had been playing racquetball, and our older son accidentally hit our youngest son in the mouth with his racquet, and it ripped his lip open. A trip to the emergency department, and a few stitches later, we were able to go home and settle down. Obviously, there are worse accidents that people experience, but having an attitude of "remain calm", in this instance, helped us to have peace, for sure.

Have you ever contemplated what you'd do if a freak accident happened to you or a loved one? What comes to mind if you stop and do this? Does your mind then go to preparing for how you will respond?

Disability/Sickness

This category can be much like the accident category. It is not necessarily your fault. I know a wife who is more like a nurse to her husband because of his health issues and disabilities. This is not the life she expected.

However, contemplating the fact that bad things *can* happen, and choosing to walk in a positive attitude, will be like putting on shoes of peace.

Unplanned Pregnancy

I know this one is a very sticky subject for a lot of people. I pray God will lead you to His truth. I know people who've been married and had an unplanned pregnancy, just like I know people who weren't married and had one.

We might even know someone who is the result of an unplanned pregnancy. In every field, in ways small and large, adoptees change the world every day. Here are a few famous people who were adopted as a result of an unplanned pregnancy:

- Faith Hill, country singer
- Nicole Kidman, actress
- Bill Clinton, former President
- Jesse Jackson, civil rights activist
- Maya Angelou, poet
- Kristin Chenoweth, Broadway star/actress
- Edgar Allen Poe, revolutionary author
- Steve Jobs, founder of Apple
- Jamie Foxx, actor and R&B star
- John Lennon, Beatles member[16]

Now, while some of these people you may or may not be a fan of, there is no doubt each person on this short list has made an impact in the world. Choosing to respond to an unplanned pregnancy positively is choosing to walk in peace. It may involve considering adoption, changing your lifestyle, etc., but having the right mindset is vital in your response to this unexpected event. Can you choose to walk in peace amid uncertainty?

Financial Change

I debated on putting financial loss here, but after giving this one some thought, I realized that a huge change financially could be unexpected, and you may need to at least consider the possibilities. Have you ever seen the reality shows about the lottery changing someone's life? I've noticed most are not for the better. Have you ever heard of a family fortune changing an entire family because of people fighting over money or possessions?

I lived through the 2008 financial crisis. It was terrible to see how some who were prepared to retire no longer could at the time they'd planned. I've also seen people lose everything to a bad investment. Sometimes, it is one's own fault, and sometimes it isn't. In some instances. People are one major health issue away from bankruptcy.

While I firmly believe in being debt-free, living within your means, and having savings for tough times, I also believe you have to be intentional about not making money a personal idol. The love of money will destroy you and your relationships and will NOT bring you peace. Putting on the shoes and preparing for times of financial changes involves obeying what God's word says about money (not making it an idol, being a cheerful giver, tithing, and living within your means). Finally, putting on the shoes of peace involves having faith that God will give you peace if you obey Him.

Job Loss

This is a separate category from money because it's deeper than that for most people; especially men. Our occupations are often tied to our identity. I've met many depressed individuals, struggling couples, and devastated business leaders or company owners who were dealing with job loss. It is tragic, for many.

I'll never forget the day my husband came home from work WAY too early, as in, before I went to work. It was in the aftermath of the 2008 crash, and he worked in construction management, which then, was basically like a job death sentence. In less than an hour, our world changed. Within two weeks, my husband decided to go back to school for engineering, though he already had a business degree. I had to go back to work full-time with a nine-month-old.

I realize, for many, this is a present-day reality, but at the time, I worked part-time and was enjoying having the best of both worlds. Sending my son to full-time daycare was almost unbearable. But you know what? I survived, and so did my son. God led us to a great place where a grandmotherly lady would rock him every morning from 6:30-7 a.m. I probably wouldn't have done that if I had been at home with him.

God also placed a precious couple from church in our lives who mentored us when we were young and newly married. This man has been like a father or spiritual father, in many ways, to my husband. During the job loss situation, Todd helped my husband get a job at the company where he worked. To have peace during this very challenging time in our lives, we had to pull up our bootstraps, allow others to help us, be open-minded, and decide to walk it out in peace, no matter how hard it was.

Relational Hurt

I define relational hurt as being wounded by loved ones from an unexpected event/comment/trial or by being misunderstood or having unmet expectations (which I would argue is the true leading cause of divorce or any relationship ending in hurt).

My, how I have been here. I truly try to be someone who fights to do the right things, and I try to love others well. Sadly, in my attempt to live this way, some haven't always seen my heart, and when they don't and lash out, it hurts. Don't get me wrong; I know God has allowed many situations to lead me to a greater place spiritually, but it's still painful.

These experiences hurt because they were unexpected. I believed people would think like I did and would know my heart automatically, but unfortunately, they didn't. People are often irrational and come at you swinging before considering your intent.

Recently, I told someone I was praying for this person's family, and the person asked me not to and to leave them alone. It hurt. I didn't understand it, at all. However, I had to choose not to stay in that place of hurt. I had to decide to move forward and not look back, to shake the dust off my feet and move on to the next person God wanted me to encourage and love, or else I wouldn't be walking in peace.

Divorce

In my experience, divorce is the death of a relationship, and it can be extra complicated because the other person is still alive. Let me first say, God loves you even if you've been divorced. God hates divorce, not you. In all of my years of counseling, I've met some amazing people who were divorced, some not by their choosing. Actually, I truly believe most people don't go into a marriage with the idea of getting divorced. We live in a broken world, however, so divorce exists.

Divorce can be devastating, especially if it is unexpected, which is often the case for one of the parties involved. It is painful. It can be very ugly and expensive. Yet, as a human in a fallen world, I believe that if I am not the wife God calls me to be, and/or if my husband isn't the husband God calls him to be, our relationship could end in this way.

In this instance, I suggest preparing to be an amazing spouse, so hopefully, divorce isn't in your future. Sadly, I realize that even if you are amazing and honor God in your marriage, divorce may still happen. One thing you can do to put on peace is to remember you, not your spouse, ultimately stands before God to give an account of *your* actions. Never say never! If you have the wrong mindset, you will not work as hard, and you won't be prepared for the unexpected. Instead say, "I will fight as hard as I can to prevent divorce, but if it happens, I will put on the shoes of peace and honor God in every response."

Good Ways to Prepare for the Unexpected

In the above scenarios, I've mentioned some major life experiences that often catch people off guard. Putting on peace is a way to be on guard, at all times, as you firmly place your faith in Jesus. The gospel of peace assures us that no matter what, God has provided us a way to have a relationship with someone who will never hurt us, even in a broken world. Below are a few strategies that can help you prepare for the unexpected:

1. Plan your attitude for the day each morning. Consider having a morning mindset that you recite. Before you get out of bed, decide to walk in peace, no matter what the day may bring. This builds resiliency.

2. Think about the hard things in life, and consider what you need to do, if at all possible, to prepare (savings, a will, etc.). Consider the "what ifs". Imagine the worst happening but also imagine the best happening. Remember, nothing ever happens exactly the way you think it will.

3. Surround yourself with supportive, helpful, and loving people who can aid you in various situations and circumstances at a moment's notice.

4. Don't over-prepare. Trust God; this is an act of faith. You don't necessarily need to hoard food, build a bomb shelter, or pack your suitcase too full.

5. Help others prepare. Talk to your family and friends

Shoes as a "Push Present" — Preparing for the Unexpected

and *especially* talk to your kids about everything. Think about the things your kids will go through in life. God showed me years ago that you cannot protect your children from everything, but *you can* prepare them, to the best of your ability, for most things.

While we can't always prepare for what happens, we can practice and prepare for our responses to circumstances and situations by considering how our actions impact others. We can prepare by being intentional, as we put on the shoes of peace, by loving those who are different than us—listening to them, and seeking to understand them. Have you done this lately? Have you given someone new or different a chance?

Journal Activity: Preparing to Walk in Peace by Considering My Biggest Fears

Think and write about your biggest fears. Consider all the possibilities of your fears coming true.

Next, consider the possibility of the opposite of your fears coming true. Writing these things out helps you to process in your mind what you are feeling and can help you see that some things aren't worth being fearful of.

Finally, assign verses to your main fears. Commit to praying these verses over your fears, daily. Write out prayers of faith.

I CAN DO ANYTHING IN THE RIGHT PAIR OF SHOES

Bible verses on planning and preparing to walk in peace with God:

The heart of man plans his way, but the Lord establishes his steps.
Proverbs 16:9, ESV

Commit your work to the Lord, and your plans will be established.
Proverbs 16:3, ESV

But all things should be done decently and in order.
1 Corinthians 14:40, ESV

Come now, you who say, "Today or tomorrow we will go into such and such a town and spend a year there and trade and make a profit"— yet you do not know what tomorrow will bring. What is your life? For you are a mist that appears for a little time and then vanishes. Instead you ought to say, "If the Lord wills, we will live and do this or that."
James 4:13-14, ESV

For which of you, desiring to build a tower, does not first sit down and count the cost, whether he has enough to complete it?
Luke 14:28, ESV

The plans of the diligent lead surely to abundance, but everyone who is hasty comes only to poverty.
Proverbs 21:5, ESV

Go to the ant, O sluggard; consider her ways, and be wise. Without having any chief, officer, or ruler, she prepares her bread in

Shoes as a "Push Present" — Preparing for the Unexpected

summer and gathers her food in harvest.
Proverbs 6:6-8, ESV

*In all your ways acknowledge him, and
he will make straight your paths.*
Proverbs 3:6, ESV

*Prepare your work outside; get everything
ready for yourself in the field, and after
that build your house.*
Proverbs 24:27, ESV

*But seek first the kingdom of God and his righteousness
and all these things will be added to you.*
Matthew 6:33, ESV

*As the heavens are higher than the earth, so are my ways
higher than your ways and my thoughts than your thoughts.*
Isaiah 55:9, ESV

*May he give you the desire of your heart
and make all your plans succeed.*
Psalm 20:4, ESV

*Plans fail for lack of counsel, but with
many advisers they succeed.*
Proverbs 15:22, ESV

***I can walk in peace by being more proactive in planning,
to respond with peace instead of being reactive!***

SEVEN

The High Heel Weapon —Navigating Conflicts

. . . Make me walk on my high heels.
— Habakkuk 3:19, (my spin on this verse)

Please do not judge me unfairly . . . Yes, I have considered using my heels as a weapon, and this is a big deal for me because I have loved high heels since I was a little girl in the 1980s. High heels, in the 1980s, came in all colors, and my Aunt Gloria, my dad's older sister, had every color including lime green and hot pink. As a kid, I thought her closet was where you prepared to walk on streets of gold. She is my dad's older sister, and my sisters and I were among the younger of the kids in the family. Her children were grown when she and my uncle Donnie used to babysit us, so they enjoyed having little girls around to bring adventure to the house. Aunt Gloria wore high heels to work and church, but she still let me play dress up in them. She knew, as soon as I got to her house, I would run straight to her closet and put on some of her high heels. This memory still brings me joy.

Even today, with feet that are different sizes, I will buy two pairs of shoes to be able to successfully wear high heels. So, as you can imagine, the fact that I would consider taking one or two off to fight someone is a big deal. Thankfully, I haven't had to so far in life. I hope and pray I never have to use them, or anything else for that matter, as a weapon for self-defense, but the chances are higher for me than others, as I have never been one to run from conflict.

Recently, we have all been tortured by news about our experiences with political unrest, racial divides, the pitting of religious people vs. LGBTQIA+, pro-choice and other groups, gas shortages, wars in the world . . . the list, sadly, goes on. I almost took some frustrating matters into my own hands during a gas shortage when a girl cut in line, after I had patiently waited for thirty minutes. Against my better judgment, at the time, I confronted her, kindly telling her it was rude to cut in line. She began cursing me out in front of everyone and left me considering whether or not I would need to use my high heels as weapons. Many people avoid conflict thinking it will magically go away or no longer exist if we just ignore it. However, others go into conflict ready to fight. We can't put on peace by avoiding conflicts or by aggressively fighting through them. Although you may be like me, who used to deal with conflicts like a bull in a china shop, you can learn to embrace difficult moments by seeking peace.

The lady who cut in line didn't like me asking her to think of others. She proceeded to cuss at me and threatened to fight me. Her reasoning for cutting in line was that she was almost out of gas. I guess she didn't consider the fact that the line of people she cut in front of was likely in the same position. At any rate, I upset her so much, she followed me after we left. I guess she wasn't too worried about wasting gas at that point. Eventually, I pulled into a church parking lot (why not?) and was blessed to find a police officer sitting there. I spoke to him, and he kindly addressed her because she had pulled into the church parking lot right after me.

As I look back on this situation, conflict can seem silly, at times. If I had only prayed and asked God how to respond to this woman, or if I should at all, I might have been able to address the conflict more productively. Later on, praying through the situation, God spoke to me and said, "If you had asked me, I would have told you to buy her gas and not say a word about cutting. Let Me work on her." This was still addressing the issue, but it would've allowed God to show me how to respond. I really wish I had been slower in my anger. I can only imagine what that might have done for her heart.

Like most, I could rationalize my nature. Maybe it's because I had to be a fighter, having been born with a disability. I had to work harder to walk, play, and look cool growing up. I'm also a middle child, so as not to be forgotten (mom . . . just kidding), I had to fight. Sometimes, I call my parents to see if they remember me, and when I say, "Hi, Mom. It's Natalie," my mom often responds with "Who?" as a joke. I love her sarcasm.

Alternatively, you may be someone who just avoids conflict, and you may have your own rationale for why you do. I'm not saying you should be someone who starts fights or tries to always have drama by creating conflict. However, I am saying that you can't avoid it. If you do, at some point, it will likely blow up in your face. If I had listened to God at the gas station, I'd have responded differently. God wasn't asking me to let it go. He was asking me to respond to my frustration in love.

I realize that, unlike me, most people dislike conflict. Don't get me wrong; I don't like having an issue with someone. I just like it being resolved. To me, addressing the conflict leads to the ultimate goal, which is resolution. People who don't like conflict often get stuck in the feelings associated with conflict, or the actions they foresee such as yelling or fighting. They often forget that conflict can be helpful by encouraging individuals to have a deeper understanding of one another. Dealing with conflict allows each person to be heard and express their true feelings and thoughts.

I CAN DO ANYTHING IN THE RIGHT PAIR OF SHOES

Think about those people in your life who like to deal with issues and resolve them. If you are not like them, I imagine they can annoy you to a certain extent, but I bet if you think about it, you probably always know where you stand with these people. Isn't there something positive to be said about this? Addressing conflict can help you and the other person understand one another's boundaries, beliefs, morals, concerns, and more. Walking in peace involves, at times, making peace with others by dealing with conflict. These things will allow you to build a better relationship. However, not addressing conflict can lead to some very harmful behaviors. Let's think about how not addressing conflict can lead to major concerns.
Consider the impact of not bringing up concerns about the following (These are just a few examples . . .):

Bullying

Oftentimes, bullying continues because no one says anything or because no one helps the person who brings up the concern. It can be damaging to a person physically, mentally, and spiritually. When I was a high school counselor, I had students come in often to discuss concerns related to bullying. I also remember being bullied at one point in my life for having an accident at school. If we don't bring up concerns or deal with concerns brought to our attention surrounding bullying, grave consequences can result.

Self-harm

Sadly, more and more people harm themselves. Some think self-harm is a release of pain, but ultimately, it is a sign of deep hurt that needs to be dealt with as soon as possible. If no one ever brings up a concern or tries to get the person who is harming him or herself to help, the unimaginable could happen. So, make sure you don't avoid the conflict of bringing up a concern about someone you love.

Sexual Abuse

Have you ever heard of the "cycle of abuse"? How do you think the cycle ends if no one ever addresses it? By addressing a tough situation with me, and my older sister, and by dealing with family conflict, my parents respected us, gave us confidence in being able to raise our concerns, showed us justice, and saved us from additional abuse.

A Dangerous Relationship

This could range from a negative friendship to an abusive partner. To get out of a dangerous relationship, you can not ignore the conflicts that caused the danger. You have to see it for what it is and address it, which may simply be by setting good boundaries or by ending the relationship. Either way, the conflict is addressed and not avoided.

People in Potentially Dangerous Situations

So many people think situations are "not my business," yet, they stalk people online on social media for hours. If someone is in danger, and you are made aware of the situation, it is your business. Speak up.

Have you ever heard of the NASA Challenger accident in 1986? How about the devastation of Chernobyl?

I remember learning about a term called "groupthink" when I was in college learning about the Challenger Disaster of 1986. It is a concept describing a "mode of thinking in which individual members of small cohesive groups tend to accept a viewpoint or conclusion that represents a perceived group consensus, whether or not the group members believe it to be valid, correct, or optimal."[17]

In January 1986, the Challenger blew up in seventy-three seconds and killed seven people. There was pressure from some engineers, NASA, and others involved to get the orbiter into space at a specific time and appease the government and public. There was one person concerned about something seemingly small. A big enough deal *wasn't* made of it to ensure it was fixed. According to Amt Teitel of history.com, "O-ring was known to be sensitive to the cold and could only work above 53 degrees. The temperature on the launch pad that morning was 36 degrees." I cannot imagine knowing there was a problem and not screaming, "No; they can't go yet!"

Have you ever been a part of a group, team, church committee, board, volunteer group, etc., and consented, either directly or indirectly, to something that led to a very bad or flawed decision?

Later in the article, Teitel again states, "The Commission ultimately flagged the root cause of the accident as "a serious flaw in the decision-making process leading up to the launch."[18]

Strangely enough, it was also in 1986, just a few short months after the Challenger tragedy, that a reactor at the Chernobyl Nuclear Power Plant in Ukraine exploded. "There were design flaws, there were decades of ignored warnings of minor failures and discovered flaws, there was human error on the night of the accident itself, and then there was the secrecy that, you know, ran through everything in the Soviet Union and the atomic industry, in particular, that complicated and exacerbated all of the foregoing three problems," says Adam Higginbotham, a journalist and author of *Midnight in Chernobyl*. "And it was this chain of events that really went back 10 to 20 years that ultimately resulted in the accident on April 26th," he said. As a result, thirty-one people died that day, and many others in the aftermath, as a result of the radioactive materials from the worst nuclear accident in history.[19]

Can you imagine being a part of the leadership in that power plant ten to twenty years before the explosion? I realize not all conflict avoidance will lead to a disaster such as the Challenger, but why risk any disaster?

Have you ever said or thought, "I wish I had said something . . . " You may not think addressing conflict can be life or death, but in these cases, it was.

I strongly believe putting on shoes of peace involves addressing conflict. Satan wants you to believe there is peace when there isn't, at times. Ezekiel 13:10 says, "Because they lead my people astray, saying, 'Peace,' when there is no peace…" Satan, at times, uses a sense of false peace. He may even trick you into believing you shouldn't address a conflict to keep the peace. Keeping a false sense of peace is NOT what God called us to. God calls us to be peacemakers. Peace isn't the absence of conflict; it involves trusting the Lord and doing the right thing in the midst of it. Peace comes from the Lord; as Psalm 29:11, ESV says, "The Lord blesses his people with peace."

So How Did Jesus Handle Conflict?

For we do not have a high priest who is unable to sympathize with our weaknesses, but we have one who was tempted in every way that we are, yet was without sin.
Hebrews 4:15, ESV

Jesus dealt with his parents' struggles, siblings, work, friends, enemies, government, religions, and the law, but He did so without sinning. Dealing with conflict is not something we should avoid. Jesus didn't avoid it!

Just this morning, I was reading in John 19, about the conflict surrounding His death. Pilate was in turmoil over doing what the Jews wanted him to do to Jesus versus what he thought was the right thing to do. His wife even told him not to kill Jesus, as a result of a dream.

I love the exchange mentioned in John 19:7-12, NKJV: "The leaders answered, 'We have a law that says he should die, because he said he is the Son of God.'

When Pilate heard this, he was even more afraid. He went back inside the palace and asked Jesus, 'Where do you come from?' But Jesus did not answer him. Pilate said, 'You refuse to speak to me? Don't you know I have power to set you free and power to have you crucified?'

Jesus answered, 'The only power you have over me is the power given to you by God. The man who turned me in to you is guilty of a greater sin.'"

Jesus didn't run from the conflict. Jesus was quiet when he needed to be, as he let Pilate think about the first question he'd asked. Yet, after the second one, when the conversation seemed to become a bit more intense, Jesus responded to Pilate's fear with truth, by saying, "The only power you have over me is the power given to you by God . . . " BOOM. (John left the mic-dropping boom out of the narrative). Jesus died for us as a result of the conflict of sin. If Jesus had avoided conflict, we would all die without a chance to be reconciled to God.

We can learn a great deal from Jesus, as we study how he dealt with conflict. Here are a few things I'm learning:

1. **He listened first**. Jesus listened to Pilate first. He didn't respond immediately, which gave Pilate a chance to think, even if it made him uncomfortable. He gives everyone a chance to draw near to Him and think about

our actions. Listening in times of conflict and giving others time to think is another way we can be like Jesus.

2. **He responded in love and truth, not emotion.** He examined the need to respond or to remain silent. He didn't respond to the first question, but He did to the next one. Responding in love first involves examining if we need to respond or not to the comment, conversation, or conflict at hand. Examine the issue first so you respond as Jesus did——with love and truth, not emotion.

3. **He forgave all.** This is tough but important. Jesus died once, for all. Romans 6:10, ESV, says, "For the death he died, he died to sin, once for all, but the life he lives he lives to God." Jesus forgave us all by dying for us. We don't have to die for others to forgive us, but oftentimes, it feels like we'd rather die than forgive someone. At least, this is how we can act at times. We must remember we forgive because we have been forgiven. Forgiveness is a great way to respond to conflict. Jesus had a conflict with us, so he forgave us by dying for us. He didn't let our sins go unpunished; He just took our punishment. Therefore, if He can forgive, can't we?

4. **He reconciles with those who confess their sin and choose to follow Him.** If we've tried to deal with conflict the right way (in truth and love), then we can seek to reconcile with those with whom we have conflict. Reconciliation may not be possible in all situations, but it is worth a try.

5. **Jesus was focused on peacemaking, not peacekeeping.** There is a difference. Jesus preached, "Blessed are the peacemakers, for they shall be called sons of God" (Matthew 5:9, ESV). You can't make peace unless you do something, and often, this involves resolving con-

flict. You don't have to make peace if it is already there, so think about it. Being a peacemaker is most likely about resolving conflicts. I haven't read anywhere that God wants us to be peacekeepers, which, to me, means avoiding conflict. Loving others and walking in peace, at times, involves dealing with conflicts.

When you decide to address a conflict, here are a few things to consider:

1. **Consider what the conflict is really about.** Is it about your feelings being hurt, your identity being challenged, an injustice you feel, etc.? Ultimately, when you consider what it is really about, conflict can be like a view into what really matters to you. Accept that the other person may or may not be considering the heart of the matter like you are.

2. **Consider why you are stuck and if you want to get unstuck**. If not, go back and work on #1.

3. **Speak truth in love** by restating or summarizing the other person's concern or position AFTER you've listened to the other person. This is a great way to show you truly are listening to the other person and that you care what he or she is saying.

4. **Be aware of your nonverbal communication**. Consider your facial expressions, tone of voice, eye contact, and body language. This shows the other person you truly care and want to resolve the issue. Give the person your full attention; don't be on your phone or watching TV, etc. Think about it: if you roll your eyes, what are you saying to the other person?

5. **Use encouraging words and phrases as you are listening**. Don't be dismissive. Validate the other person.

The High Heel Weapon—Navigating Conflicts

For example, say, "Thank you for taking the time to talk with me," or "I appreciate you letting me know how this made you feel or what your position on the matter is. I hear what you are trying to say (without saying "but"). This helps the other person not feel the need to defend themselves. It shows that his or her thoughts matter to you. If you dismiss the person, then he or she will shut down and the conflict may likely remain. Becoming a good listener is very important in being able to resolve conflicts.

6. **Use "I statements"**, and don't just say, "You made me . . ., etc." Instead, try saying, "I felt . . . when . . . happened. This also helps to keep the lines of communication open and doesn't sound accusatory. However, it still allows for you to speak truth.

7. **Use silence appropriately**. Just as Jesus didn't respond at first and allowed Pilate to think, you can do the same. This allows people's emotions to not get too heated. It gives people time to think and breathe.

8. **Reflect on positive things the person has done for or with you**. Don't try to turn the focus back on yourself. Keeping things positive is a great way to speak truth in love. If you pray and think long and hard enough, you can find something positive to say.

9. **Keep the conversation moving in a positive direction**. Redirect if necessary. If the conversation takes a negative turn, take a deep breath and think about how to turn it back around in a positive direction. If it seems impossible, consider tabling the discussion when all parties involved are calmer or able to be positive.

10. **Be aware of communication blockers** such as sarcasm, globalizing, accusing, judging, insulting, unsolicited advice, diagnosing, blaming, threats, disinterest

by changing the subject, and seeking reassurance. Keep communication positive, open, and loving but still truthful.

Addressing conflict can lead to beautiful things.

"Conflicts are a lot like icebergs. What we see on the surface may seem small, but what's underneath can send boats like the Titanic to the bottom of the ocean, and if I don't pay attention to what's underneath my own conflicts it can rip holes in my relationships."[20]

As you begin to effectively address and handle conflicts, you likely will see that your communication is more effective with others, trust increases, relationships deepen, and love multiplies. Conflict resolution, not conflict avoidance, leads to peace.

Verses to meditate on dealing with conflict.

If your brother sins against you, go and tell him his fault, between you and him alone. If he listens to you, you have gained your brother. But if he does not listen, take one or two others along with you, that every charge may be established by the evidence of two or three witnesses. If he refuses to listen to them, tell it to the church. And if he refuses to listen even to the church, let him be to you as a Gentile and a tax collector.
Matthew 18:15-17, ESV

Let all bitterness and wrath and anger and clamor and slander be put away from you, along with all malice. Be kind to one another, tenderhearted, forgiving one another, as God in Christ forgave you.
Ephesians 4:31-32, ESV

The High Heel Weapon—Navigating Conflicts

*A soft answer turns away wrath,
but a harsh word stirs up anger.*
Proverbs 15:1, ESV

*Bearing with one another and, if one has a complaint
against another, forgiving each other; as the Lord
has forgiven you, so you also must forgive.*
Colossians 3:13, ESV

*What causes quarrels and what causes fights among
you? Is it not this, that your passions are at war within
you? You desire and do not have, so you murder. You
covet and cannot obtain, so you fight and quarrel. You
do not have, because you do not ask. You ask and do
not receive, because you ask wrongly, to spend it on
your passions. You adulterous people! Do you not know
that friendship with the world is enmity with God?
Therefore whoever wishes to be a friend of the world
makes himself an enemy of God. Or do you suppose
it is to no purpose that the Scripture says, "He yearns
jealously over the spirit that he has made to dwell in us"? ...*
James 4:1-6, ESV

*Be angry and do not sin; do not let the
sun go down on your anger...*
Ephesians 4:26, ESV

*Pay attention to yourselves! If your brother sins,
rebuke him, and if he repents, forgive him...*
Luke 17:3, ESV

**I can walk in peace, not by avoiding conflicts,
but by seeking to resolve conflicts.**

EIGHT

Go-to Shoes—Considering Your Relationships

"Rather than books, you have a shoe library."
—Anna Dello Russo, Italian journalist and fashion editor[21]

For many reasons, my "go-to" shoes are my running shoes or my Birkenstocks. They are comfortable, versatile, easy to slip on and take off, durable, and can be fun. When I went to India on a mission trip years ago, my Birks were the only shoes I took. They proved to be durable, for sure.

My "go-to" relationships are similar and depend on the situation I'm experiencing. If I need a laugh, I call a friend. If I need support for anything, I call another. Secrets belong to my sister. Of course, for money, I go to my husband—just kidding, *kinda*. Seriously, I go to him for almost everything. But really, we should go to the Lord for everything *first*. Who we go to first is often influenced by our past hurts in relationships. At one time or another, we've all struggled with relationships. In fact, most of our hurt comes from relationships. However, the encouraging news is, so does our healing. Contemplating relationships you need to foster, work on, or set aside, is vital in developing a peaceful walk.

When I was in high school, I was in The Miss Merry Christmas Pageant. It was my first and only beauty and talent contest. My mother regularly reminded my sisters and me that

I CAN DO ANYTHING IN THE RIGHT PAIR OF SHOES

she didn't need a pageant to tell anyone her daughters were beautiful, but this pageant was a fun thing for senior girls to participate in at my high school. The whole ordeal consisted of talent, certain outfits like sportswear, formal gown, interviews, and most importantly, BIG hair.

One of my best friends (to this day), Candice, and I almost got into a fight over having the same BIG hair professional. In a small town in the south, during the 1990s, these professionals specialized in "Jesus hair," meaning, as my friend says, the bigger it is, the closer one is to Heaven.

Thankfully, Candice and I were able to move past having to share the BIG hair professional and were able to have fun and cheer for one another during the pageant. One of the most selfless things Candice has ever done for me was to let me borrow her heels during the pageant. Now, remember, I don't wear the same size, so it was a struggle for me to walk in shoes that didn't fit at least one of my feet. I'm not even sure why I needed to borrow her shoes, but I did nonetheless. It was a struggle to walk, balance the extra hair spray on top of my head, and look like all was right with the world, as I hobbled in these shoes.

Candice rightfully won Miss Congeniality, and I was given the coveted prize of Third Runner Up. We have a silly podcast that we started in 2020, with these names as the title. We love to laugh about our experience in this pageant, among other things in life. Candice is one of my "go-to people," just like my "go-to shoes."

I realize you may think I'm weird that I have "go-to friends" for just about everything you'd need in life. Why not? Don't you contemplate the shoes you are going to wear each day? Doesn't each shoe technically have a purpose? You have house shoes to use for walking around your home. There are tennis shoes to wear for playing sports. We've already discussed the importance and beauty of high heels in a previous

Go-to Shoes—Considering Your Relationships

chapter. If we put this much thought into choosing shoes, why not choose who we need to "go-to" for specific things?

My process of choosing shoes to wear for the day may be strange for some, but it is a well-thought-out process nonetheless. To some degree, I have to because of my feet issues. I have to think about what activities I am going to be doing for the day. If I work out, certain shoes obviously apply. If I'm working in my office, I need shoes with heels to help my posture and back because I'm on the shorter side and my feet don't touch the ground comfortably. If I'm singing at church, I want shoes that look nice, aren't too flashy, but are also somewhat comfortable.

I wish I could tell you that I think about my interactions with people each day like I do my shoes, but it's not quite that simple. Be that as it may, it is important to contemplate who you should "go to" for certain things in life. Contemplating your go-to relationships before certain circumstances can help you prevent some hurts and frustrations. Of course, just like the process I have for deciding what shoe to wear for what occasions, figuring out your "go-to" relationships is somewhat of a trial-and-error process.

Biblical View of Relationships

God is all ABOUT relationships. He created us specifically to be in a relationship with Him! God created man in His own image so we could share in His creation. He wasn't lonely, nor did He need us, but He wanted us. We were created for relationship; God walked with Adam and Eve in the garden.

The Lord God said, "It is not good for the man to be alone. I will make a helper suitable for him."
Genesis 2:18, ESV

I CAN DO ANYTHING IN THE RIGHT PAIR OF SHOES

The fall of man in the beginning was ultimately about a fall in relationship. When Adam and Eve sinned, it changed the relationship with God, so we had to find a way to make things right. However, according to the Bible, we couldn't make the relationship right on our own. We needed a perfect sacrifice. So, God sent his son, Jesus, to die for us so that we might have a way back to a right relationship with Him. Romans 5:6-16 ESV (emphasis added) says, "When we were unable to help ourselves, at the moment of our need, Christ died for us."

Although many faiths and religions today teach that you can be righteous by doing good works, Christianity teaches that nothing we could do could make us right with God. It is only through Jesus and His sacrificial death that we can have a relationship with God. We must accept Jesus as our Savior, and when we do, a relationship is possible with God. Unlike most religions, following Christ and the true gospel of the Bible is about a relationship with God, not a religion.

He created others to walk alongside us *in addition* to Himself. Psalm 68:6 tells us that God sets the lonely in families. He also blesses us with other relationships than can be an extension of our relationship with him. Consider David and Johnathan. They were not only brothers-in-law but also best friends. God gave them an amazing friendship that He used to help both of them through many difficult and challenging times.

On the other hand, we have the example of Job and his friends. While Job's friends didn't always get it right, they did sit with Job during the most heart-wrenching time of his life. Job 2:13, ESV says, "Then they sat on the ground with him for seven days and seven nights. No one said a word to him, because they saw how great his suffering was." When was the last time your friends did this?

Read the Bible and you will learn about so many fascinating relationships. You will also be encouraged that while

God gives us those in the natural world to help us, He also surrounds us with supernatural support. Hebrews 12:1, ESV says, "Therefore, since we are surrounded by such a great cloud of witnesses, let us throw off everything that hinders and the sin that so easily entangles. And let us run with perseverance the race marked out for us." As a runner, I especially love this verse. I know what it means to have people cheering you on during a race. Some miles are easy. Some are fun. Some are long. Some miles are hard and honestly just suck! We need perseverance to run the race of life. Stop and thank God for those He has surrounded you with that you can't see but you know are there, cheering you on and supporting you!

Now, let's discuss the types of relationships beneficial for one to have.

People who love you for who you are.

Most likely, these are your family members, possibly your chosen family members, such as close friends or church family. These relationships are the ones you can be with while wearing the worst clothes, stinking, having no makeup on, etc. They love you just the same. I am blessed to have many of these. This is one reason, among many, I married my husband. He lets me be me in all my weirdness. He is not threatened by me but rather appreciates all God has made me to be.

People who challenge us.

These are the people who push you to be who God created you to be. These could be spiritual mentors, work mentors, family, friends, or neighbors. Sometimes, these are people you need to seek out. Maybe it is someone who believes differently than you. These people can frustrate you, but if you allow them, they can also be people who push you to grow in magnificent ways. My grandmother used to love to argue with me, but truthfully, she just loved to challenge me to think. I have friends like this too.

People who laugh with us

This may seem obvious but I need people I can call and laugh with over a situation. I need to know they can laugh with me and not judge me. These are the individuals I call when I'm having a rough day. These are vital people you need to be able to contact at a moment's notice. Those you can laugh with can take the edge off of any crazy situation. I have many friends in this category.

People who will listen to us

Having someone who will truly listen to you is such a gift. God has blessed me with many of these friends who will listen and engage in whatever I need to talk about. Some will let me vent (not the same as gossip) without judgment, which I need at times. This also may be a professional such as a counselor. Counseling is all about a trusting relationship. I have one and need one to help me process various things I deal with in life.

People who can be affectionate with us.

Do you ever just need a hug? I often do. This isn't just about what the world has made of it, being sexual touch, which is important in marriage. Thankfully, I have many people in my life who will give me hugs when I need them. The Bible speaks of the healing power of appropriately laying hands on others. Never underestimate the power of giving someone a hug at church, the office, or anytime God is leading you to hug someone.

People who you can have fun with.

I am an adventurous person, and I LOVE to have fun and take risks at times. These people are vital. When you need to have some fun, you should have people you can call! In the phase of life that I'm in currently, this category has to include people who can also have fun with my kids. I love to hang out and play games, go on trips, etc. Life is meant to be enjoyed, and you need people you can have fun with!

People to converse with.

These are people you can call to discuss interesting things with. I am a nerd, so I love to talk about theology, the news, psychology, books, etc. You may not be a super talkative person, but you still need people with whom you can talk about a variety of topics. These are people who are not going to get bored discussing a book with you or discussing sports with you or whatever you are interested in.

People who give good advice or wisdom.

These are those people like Solomon in the Bible who you can go to for amazing advice or wisdom. There may be different ones for different matters, depending on the area in which you need advice. At work, I have to have people I can "consult" with on different clients and cases. Consultation is vital in my line of work as a counselor. Consulting with other professionals gives me new insights and applications to try with clients.

People who can pray with and for you.

I call these my prayer warriors. I'm so blessed to have a group of people who will pray with and for me whenever I need them. These people will text me prayers from time to time, pray with me during times of stress, and pray for me in general.

People who allow space, time, and the ability to be autonomous.

You need people in your life who can give you space or time and not be offended if you need quiet time, alone time, or to just sit with them in silence. Job's friends in the Old Testament sat with him in silence for seven days before they said a word. These people are also those who let you be you and don't feel the need to compete with you or change you.

People you trust and who make you feel secure.

My husband makes me feel safe, and I know I can trust him. He also knows I'll *hurt* him if he breaks my trust. He is a big, muscular dude and has been since I've known him. However, he has always let me be who I am and let me be independent. Sometimes he even says to people I'm scarier than he is. I did make a teacher cry once in a conference . . . that's a story for another day. When he needs to stand up for me though, he will. I'll never forget the time he told some individuals they were never allowed to speak to me again without him present because he didn't trust them to speak respectfully to me. I felt so secure at that moment. People you can trust and those who make you feel secure don't need to have muscles, but they do need to have the ability to make you feel safe and cared for. I also know that my husband is a great provider and good at managing money, while also looking to God as the ultimate leader of our family.

People who make you feel like a priority.

I hope and pray you have people in your life who you feel will drop anything for you. These may also be those people who will make you a meal or buy you a gift just to show you they are thinking about you and that you are a priority to them. My running friends, who are some of my best friends, truly always make me feel like I'm a priority. When you agree to run up a mountain and back down for a total of twenty miles with someone or do a crazy ten-mile Spartan run, trust me; you are a priority to those people!

People who you can connect with.

These are people who you feel a shared sense of meaning with. For me, it is often those with struggles with their feet or those who experienced a similar struggle that I have in life. Connection concerning a shared experience is why group therapy can work beautifully.

Honorable Mentions

People who would likely bail you out of jail.

These are those people you can call when you may have done something stupid, and you need their help, without judgment.

People who will help you hide a body.

These are the people who will, not literally, help you murder someone and/or cover it up. Rather, these are the people who will listen to you and get angry with you, but they won't let you stay there.

People who will fight for you.

These are people who get angry at those who mistreat you. My older sister always threatens to smear lipstick over anyone who has hurt me. She is not a fighter in the physical sense, so this is a joke to those who know her love. However, there is something comforting about her sending me a lipstick emoji in response to my telling her I was upset.

While considering your repertoire of "Go-To Relationships", consider the following:

No one person will provide all of your needs outside of Jesus. Never expect anyone but Jesus to be your savior, your all, your hope, your promise for a bright future. When we put this pressure on others, we will always be hurt by others falling short of our expectations. For example, if your hope for a bright future is in your children, you may impose unnecessary and unfair expectations on them to fulfill the things in life that you want. This is not necessarily what God wants for them.

Some people fit into multiple categories. Don't look at this list and think, wow, I don't know that many people or I don't have that many friends. First of all, always keep your heart and mind open to making new friends and letting some go, but remember that some people fit into more than one of these "go-to" categories.

Go-to Shoes—Considering Your Relationships

Don't believe the lie that you are okay all by yourself. You weren't created to be alone. If a global pandemic and stay-at-home orders taught us anything, surely, this was one of those lessons. The Bible says in Proverbs 27:17, NIV: "As iron sharpens iron, so one person sharpens another."

Payback, and pay it forward. Be a "go-to" friend for people. Be open to loving others and helping others. Recently, I heard a Christian author and speaker suggest that we put up walls to ward off people. When you've been hurt or disappointed by people, you want to put up walls, but if you do, you may be shutting out Jesus, as He uses others to minister to you. Also, be available for others by spending time with them one-on-one or in groups, in person.

Write down your go-to's. Pray for them and their families. Journal about them and express gratitude. Bless them often by doing things for them such as sending a handwritten note, baking a cake, simply hugging them, or sitting down for a chat in their office. Set up group texts for your prayer warriors or different needs (funny meme group, running group, prayer warrior group, etc.).

Remember some relationships are seasonal. As the old saying goes, make new friends, and keep the old; one is silver and the other gold. Some people are not supposed to be in your life long term. Accept this, and keep moving forward.

View relationships, at times, like playing on a sports team. You are playing in the game of life. Some relationships need to be sidelined for a while. Some need to be taken out of your game due to a personal foul. Some need to be kicked out of the stadium forever. Some will play for a while, then go to another team to play. Some will fight with you until the end.

Don't force people to be your "go-to" in any category. Not every person is the "go-to" for every situation. Carefully examining the right "go-to" person, at the right time, will help you walk in peace. Remember this may change depending on what you need in the moment.

Consider loving others with all of the love languages: affection, quality time, gifts, acts of service, and words of affirmation. I like to add "food." Maybe it's a Southern thing, but some good food can cover a lot of hurts . . . maybe that's why it's called a "covered dish" in the South! Finally, forgive those who've hurt you, and don't let hurt, or the potential for hurt, stop you from trying again with people. Forgiveness is love, and it needs to be a part of all the love languages.

People to Stay Away From or Set Strong Boundaries:

Negative People:
We all know these. Who comes to mind right now? Don't say it aloud, but sadly, we all know one—The Debbie Downer or the Negative Nancy. It's the person you have lunch with because you feel obligated, and afterward, you feel like crap. The sky is gray no matter how bright the sun is that day and everyone is out to get them. These people are those you should pray for but do not spend a ton of time with them. If you can, speak truth to them in love but keep moving.

Miserable People:
The term misery loves company is SO true. Therefore, don't spend time with these people. These people aren't just negative, they are miserable, and for some unknown reason, they sulk in their misery.

Go-to Shoes—Considering Your Relationships

Hateful People:
These people are the ones who love to poke fun and make mean jabs any time they are around.

Bad Influences:
This isn't just for teens . . . adults can succumb to bad influences as well. I recite 1 Corinthians 15:33, often to my sons: "Do not be deceived: 'Bad company ruins good morals'", but it is also for adults. Don't be deceived by thinking it won't happen to you.

Time Suckers:
These are the people who may talk your ear off or stop in and not consider any social cues as to the fact that you are busy, need to go, get off the phone, etc. You may love this person, but beware, and set boundaries. Have an exit plan or strategy.

Lazy or Unmotivated People:
Sadly, these characteristics in people can be contagious . . . think about it. Remember the times in your life when you were the most productive? Now, think about the people you surrounded yourself with during these times. I bet they were also highly motivated individuals.

Abusers:
I'm leaving this term somewhat broad on purpose. Abusers can be anyone who takes advantage of you. It could be as simple as someone who repeatedly asks for money to someone who abuses you emotionally or physically. If you are being abused in any form, get help. These people will never change unless you change.

Pray for God to show you who needs to be your "go-

I CAN DO ANYTHING IN THE RIGHT PAIR OF SHOES

to" for different needs in your life. Pray that God will allow you to be a "go-to" for others. Finally, thank Him for His son, Jesus, and the relationship you can have with Him.

Verses to meditate on regarding relationships:

If either of them falls down,
one can help the other up.
But pity anyone who falls
and has no one to help them up.
Ecclesiastes 4:10, ESV

For this very reason, make every effort to add
to your faith goodness; and to goodness,
knowledge; and to knowledge, self-control; and
to self-control, perseverance; and to perseverance,
godliness; and to godliness, mutual affection;
and to mutual affection, love.
2 Peter 1:5-7, ESV

So in everything, do to others what you would have them
do to you, for this sums up the Law and the Prophets.
Matthew 7:12, ESV

Two are better than one, because they have
a good return for their labor.
Ecclesiastes 4:9, ESV

May the Lord make your love increase and overflow for
each other and for everyone else, just as ours does for you.
1 Thessalonians 3:12, ESV

As iron sharpens iron, so one person sharpens another.
Proverbs 27:17, ESV

Go-to Shoes—Considering Your Relationships

A friend loves at all times, and a brother is born for a time of adversity.
Proverbs 17:17, ESV

I can walk in peace by knowing who my "go-to" relationships are when I am in need.

NINE

Purple Hologram Shoes—Living in an Overstimulated World

*"It isn't the mountain ahead that wears you out;
it's the grain of sand in your shoe."*
—Robert W. Service, British-Canadian poet and writer[22]

Admittedly, I like different shoes, but I'm not sure I'd say I've ever liked "outrageous" shoes. Occasionally, I like shoes that have patterns. I like stylish shoes but purple hologram? Not so much. Most likely, some of my most outrageous shoes would probably have been worn when I was in my late teens and early twenties. I remember heels with holes in them. At times, over the years, I've seen these try to pop back up in stores, but for some reason, they don't seem to last style-wise . . . at least, not like they did in the 90s.

One of the most threatening challenges to putting on peace is overstimulation. We have phones, tablets, computers, work, small groups, traffic lights, streaming services, and purple hologram shoes, which according to Google, are on the list of the most outrageous shoes. Trust me; these shoes will stimulate something in you, hopefully not a psychedelic response. Do you know what Science says about overstimulation to your brain? The research is alarming enough to motivate us all to take action! We cannot put on peace if we are constantly overstimulated.

I CAN DO ANYTHING IN THE RIGHT PAIR OF SHOES

While I'm not quite sure any of my shoes would be considered overstimulating, my feet certainly have suffered greatly from overstimulation. After I had my second son, I decided to run my first half marathon (yes, 13.1 miles). As someone born club-footed who didn't walk until after two years of age, and someone who has asthma, this was a challenge, to say the least. The fact that my legs and feet are different sizes affects my hips, back, and entire body, as you might imagine. Therefore, I have to be fitted for the right pair of running shoes in addition to having custom orthotics. Yes; I realize this makes me sound 180 years old . . .

After months of training, I decided to run the Myrtle Beach Mini Marathon with some of my closest friends. We went down for a fun adult weekend and left the kids at home. Excited and nervous, we started early on a Saturday morning, on the beautiful coast of South Carolina, with hundreds of runners. My goal was just to finish.

Around mile nine, my body began to feel overstimulated. Well, actually, my stomach began to feel very upset. This made me nervous. In all my preparation, no one warned me about anything potentially happening to my bowels. I was thinking, I've got this! Only a 5k to go, and I had done quite a few of those at that point in my life. However, when my bowels started rumbling, my body knew that if I stopped, I would likely not be able to finish the race, so I kept going. I'm sure you are wondering if I lost control of my bowels at this point, and the answer is no. However, as I excitedly crossed the finish line and ran into my husband's arms, I felt it coming.

My husband said, "Uh, are you okay?"

To which I responded, "Nope; I just crapped myself," and he said, "Oh, let's get you to a bathroom." Being the "survivor" I like to think I am, I was developing a plan on the way to the bathroom, including washing my clothes and body in the sink of the bathroom and putting them back on wet. You gotta do what you gotta do sometimes, right?

Thankfully, when I reached the bathroom, I was thrilled to see I had not crapped my pants. I barely made it, but I made it! My body was overstimulated and not prepared for that level of running for that long.

Also, after I took my shoes off, it looked like a murder had happened to one of my toes. No one told me that I should prepare my toes for all of the rubbing that would occur.

Overstimulation in life is a bit like my first half-marathon experience. It may be happening below the surface, but until you stop or are forced to stop, you don't realize the damage that is being done. I learned after this race to use petroleum jelly between my toes and other areas of my body to prevent chafing. I also learned to fuel my body with the proper nutrition and supplements to help with a thing I didn't know at the time called "runner's diarrhea." Yes; it's a real thing. Look it up . . .

Overstimulation can be a result of overdoing it physically, mentally, spiritually, emotionally, socially, etc. Our bodies, including our minds, need rest. We are not created to handle the amount of stimulation the world would like us to believe we need any more than my body is created to run a half marathon every day.

In today's world, we have so many things stimulating our minds. A simple drive to the store can consist of lights, loud sounds, traffic, someone cutting you off, a call from your mom, tuning into a meeting via Zoom or some other online platform, or eating a snack.

Some professionals use the term "overstimulation" to describe individuals with sensory processing struggles, social struggles, or those who struggle to regulate their emotions. However, I believe we are all suffering at some level from overstimulation, as a result of technology, at least in developed nations.

I CAN DO ANYTHING IN THE RIGHT PAIR OF SHOES

Scientists have been studying the effects of technology, related to cell phones, concerning how our bodies react. The research is broad and ongoing. Research reports that "Studies are beginning to show links between smartphone usage and increased levels of anxiety and depression, poor sleep quality, and increased risk of car injury or death."[23] According to an article from Harvard, "If you've ever misplaced your phone, you may have experienced a mild state of panic until it's been found. About 73% of people claim to experience this unique flavor of anxiety, which makes sense when you consider that adults in the US spend an average of 2-4 hours per day tapping, typing, and swiping on their devices—that adds up to over 2,600 daily touches. Most of us have become so intimately entwined with our digital lives that we sometimes feel our phones vibrating in our pockets when *they aren't even there.*"[24]

Also, some suggest individuals can only connect with about 150 individuals or so. Yet, thanks to social media, we have the ability to connect with over two billion people. We cannot emotionally or socially handle what social media is making available to us.[25]

Yes; I'm on social media, and I know it has a lot of benefits. However, we must remember that to whom much is given, much is required. Social media should come with boundaries and with the understanding that there is a lot of responsibility required for successful use. Maybe there should be a training course, like training for half marathons, before signing up for an account? Just a thought.

I could go on about social media and technology and the effect they have on our brains for days, but there have already been plenty of books written on this topic. My point is, if you want to walk in peace daily, you have to realize the areas in which you are overstimulated and make some changes.

Overstimulation can also be caused by doing too much. If you know me, you know this is a struggle for me. My dad told me to slow down the other day, and I said, "Dad, you are the pot calling the kettle black." He is one of the busiest retired people I know. He is volunteering, working a job after retiring from thirty-nine years in the military, keeping grandkids, and leading a Bible study at a coffee shop, among other things. It wears me out thinking about it. However, just because I have the nature to "do too much" doesn't mean I should. I must constantly seek God to make sure that the things I am doing are the things He wants and not what I want. If I stay in God's will, then He won't overwhelm me.

Work can be overstimulating. Kids can be noisy. Trying to be an amazing spouse, volunteer, world changer, trendsetter, or anything else you feel you need to be to stand out, can be tiring. Our lives can be exhausting. I'm often reminded of an old saying, "If the devil can't make you bad, he'll make you busy." Ouch; this sure is convicting for me.

What Does Overstimulation Feel Like and How to Identify It

According to Psychology Today, overstimulation can be described as strong feelings, disparate thoughts, physical, mental, and emotional tension, and inner restlessness. Overstimulation can lead to exhaustion and tiredness as a result of one's nervous system being in overdrive for too long.[26]

Being inundated with anything related to our senses (sight, sound, touch, taste, and smells or other sensations) can lead to overstimulation because our bodies can't often cope. Our brain can't process too many things at one time.

Some signs that you are overstimulated:
- Becoming easily overwhelmed
- Not being able to regulate your emotions (crying too often, not crying when you used to be able to, getting

angry over things you shouldn't)
- Being easily rattled or nervous
- Feeling emotional exhaustion leading to a lack of empathy
- Physical exhaustion
- Struggle to focus
- Lack of motivation
- Increase in need for numbing substances

I believe the opioid crisis is due, in part, to people being overstimulated. In 2019, nearly 50,000 people in the United States died from opioid-involved overdoses.[27] People are looking to numb the pain from so many things. If we can't handle all the world expects us to, we often seek help in the wrong places. This is a tragedy.

Potential societal effects of overstimulation:
- Individuals deciding not to work like their parents
- People deciding not to have children or get married (Could it be that life is just too much for people to handle these days, so they decide not to take on more responsibility?)
- A rise in disorders such as ADHD
- Increase in car accidents (texting and driving)

Biblical Application:
If you aren't new to Bible study, especially as a female, you are likely not surprised that I'm adding this story into this chapter.

Now as they went on their way, Jesus entered a village. And a woman named Martha welcomed him into her house. And she had a sister called Mary, who sat at the Lord's feet and listened to his teaching. But Martha

was distracted with much serving. And she went up to him and said, "Lord, do you not care that my sister has left me to serve alone? Tell her then to help me." But the Lord answered her, "Martha, Martha, you are anxious and troubled about many things, but one thing is necessary. Mary has chosen the good portion, which will not be taken away from her."
Luke 10:38-42, ESV

I always felt sorry for Martha. Having sisters, I wanted to say to Mary, "Get up, and help your sister." I was taught everyone should help clean up and serve. While this may be true and respectful, this is not what the story is about here, nor is it what Jesus wants us to glean from this passage.

Martha wasn't necessarily doing anything wrong, but her focus was off, at that moment. Jesus acknowledges our service to Him, but He doesn't want us to become overstimulated by the worries of life in such a way that we miss out on spending time with Him! We can't neglect the importance of sitting at the feet of Jesus as Mary did. God promises according to Exodus 33:14, ESV, "My presence shall go with you, and I will give you rest."

In C.S. Lewis's book, *The Great Divorce*, he writes, "There have been men before now who got so interested in proving the existence of God that they came to care nothing for God Himself . . . as if the good Lord had nothing to do but exist. There have been some who were so occupied in spreading Christianity that they never gave a thought to Christ . . . Ye see it in smaller matters. Do ye never know a lover of books that with all his first editions and signed copies has lost the power to read them? Or an organizer of charities that had lost all love for the poor? It is the subtlest of all the snares."[28]

I love this passage as it reminds me to do exactly what Mary did, sit at the feet of Jesus. We need to be reminded not to become so overstimulated and overwhelmed by everything in the world, remembering that the essence of the Christian faith is about having a relationship with God, which is impossible if you never spend time with Him.

In this way, I can see how sly the devil is. He has used many of the great creations of man to keep us overstimulated and overwhelmed so that we are ineffective and forget what life is truly all about.

When was the last time you sat at the feet of Jesus? Do you spend time with Him daily? Do you silence your phone regularly to hear the Holy Spirit?

Jesus stole away often . . . He rested. He set an example for us: "And God blessed the seventh day and declared it holy, because it was the day when He rested from all His work of creation" (Genesis 2:3, ESV).

The helpful behaviors of finding balance in an overstimulated world.

- Rest and take breaks from the overstimulating things in your life.
- Relax. Take a bath in silence. Go sit on a porch and swing. Go for a walk without any technology or music.
- Be still. This is a hard one, but a good one. God commands it. Psalm 46:10, ESV, says, "Be still, and know that I am God; I will be exalted among the nations, I will be exalted in the earth."
- Be quiet. Ecclesiastes 3:7, ESV, says, "There is a time to tear and a time to mend, a time to be silent and a time to speak…"
- Set boundaries with the things that overwhelm you. Take back control. Set restrictions for your technology.

- Turn off notifications on your phone. Only look when you need to, not every time it buzzes or rings.
- Set a good example for your children. Have limits for yourself, not just them.
- Gauge your emotions, and regulate them daily.
- Remember, not all people are the same, and some can handle more than others . . .

On my second half marathon trip, some of the people we knew who were also running the race, actually biked down to the beach (which is about a four-hour drive from where we all live) and then ran the half marathon the next day. My body is getting overstimulated just thinking about that amount of physical exercise. These individuals could handle way more than I could, physically, and that is okay! We should celebrate the differences of others instead of being intimidated or letting others' talents make us believe we aren't as good as them. We can all handle different things. We should never try to be someone we aren't.

One of the girls in the bike-down group made it her goal to help me reach my personal goal of a sub-two-hour half-marathon. Though her physical fitness abilities intimidated me, she impressed me when she gave up her desire to help me attain my goal. During the race, she encouraged me and wouldn't let me give up. She even ran backward, at times, to yell encouraging words at me. She also noticed, at one point, I was shutting down because my hands were freezing, so she took off her gloves and gave them to me. This made a huge difference for me during that race. I don't see her often, but she will always hold a special place in my heart.

This leads to my next points to consider. Help others when you realize they are overstimulated or overwhelmed. If you see someone struggling, offer help. Helping others can be a way to alleviate your own stress, as long as it is what God wants you to do. Follow the spirit of truth: "When the Spirit of truth comes, he will guide you into all the truth, for he will not speak on his own authority, but whatever he hears he will speak, and he will declare to you the things that are to come" (John 16:13, ESV).

Verses to Meditate on

Go to the ant, O sluggard, Observe her ways and be wise...
Proverbs 6:6, ESV

But Martha was distracted with all her preparations; and she came up to Him and said, "Lord, do You not care that my sister has left me to do all the serving alone? Then tell her to help me."
Luke 10:40, ESV

The seed which fell among the thorns, these are the ones who have heard, and as they go on their way they are choked with worries and riches and pleasures of this life, and bring no fruit to maturity.
Luke 8:14, ESV

...and to make it your ambition to lead a quiet life and attend to your own business and work with your hands, just as we commanded you...
1 Thessalonians 4:11, ESV

For we hear that some among you are leading an undisciplined life, doing no work at all, but acting like busybodies.
2 Thessalonians 3:11, ESV

Purple Hologram Shoes—Living in an Overstimulated World

And He said to them, "Why is it that you were looking for Me? Did you not know that I had to be in My Father's house?"
Luke 2:49, ESV

But now thus says the Lord, he who created you, O Jacob, he who formed you, O Israel: "Fear not, for I have redeemed you; I have called you by name, you are mine. When you pass through the waters, I will be with you; and through the rivers, they shall not overwhelm you; when you walk through fire you shall not be burned, and the flame shall not consume you.
Isaiah 43:1-2, ESV

Come to me, all who labor and are heavy laden, and I will give you rest.
Matthew 11:28, ESV

Do not be conformed to this world, but be transformed by the renewal of your mind, that by testing you may discern what is the will of God, what is good and acceptable and perfect.
Romans 12:2, ESV

Come to me, all who labor and are heavy laden, and I will give you rest. Take my yoke upon you, and learn from me, for I am gentle and lowly in heart, and you will find rest for your souls. For my yoke is easy, and my burden is light.
Matthew 11:28-30, ESV

Do not let wisdom and understanding out of your sight, preserve sound judgment and discretion; they will be life for you, an ornament to grace your neck.

I CAN DO ANYTHING IN THE RIGHT PAIR OF SHOES

Then you will go on your way in safety, and your foot will not stumble. When you lie down, you will not be afraid; when you lie down, your sleep will be sweet.
Proverbs 3:21-24, ESV

Meditation on Psalm 61

Try reading this aloud, having a Bible app read it to you, or writing this out as you meditate on it, making it personal for your current situation.

As you do, take a deep breath and ask God to:
Hear your cry. Attend to your prayer, as it comes from the ends of the earth to Thee.

Think about the earth from sea to sea, continent to continent, and ask God to hear and attend to all of your cries, as they may feel as big as the whole earth.

Put your hand over your overwhelmed heart. Ask God to help.

Picture a massive rock, one that is much bigger than you, much higher than you. Ask God to lead you to Him.

Thank God for being a shelter and a strong tower for you from the enemy.

Take another deep breath, and feel God taking away your burdens and giving you peace.

I can walk in peace by resting and finding balance in an overstimulated environment.

TEN

Interview Shoes—Avoiding Dangerous Distractions

"So many shoes and only two feet."
—Sarah Jessica Parker, actress and producer[29]

Years ago, I had the privilege to interview someone for a counseling position at a school where I worked. The person was great on paper, but she walked in with very bright and distinct-looking shoes. These shoes were red, shiny, and platformed with a very high heel; not exactly what you expect for a job interview, at least in a school setting. I was totally distracted. It seemed odd to wear those shoes in an interview for that position and place. It took everyone on the interview committee a minute to focus on the task at hand, because we were caught off guard. We were distracted.

While bright shoes in an interview can distract someone from listening to potentially good answers to interview questions, shoes aren't necessarily dangerous distractions in and of themselves. But we all experience the most dangerous distraction in life at one time or another: stress. Not managing it leads to a ton of problems, including serious physical and mental health problems, and relational problems (compassion fatigue, burnout, and communication struggles). Putting on peace each day can alleviate the great distraction of stress because we need to be ready and on guard to preach the gospel both in season and out of season (2 Timothy 4:2). This is not the only reason for putting on peace, but it should be at the top of our list of reasons why we need to put on our shoes of peace daily.

I'm sure this isn't the first time you have read about what I call the most dangerous of distractions. For many, stress is an ongoing problem that can keep people from living a life of peace or walking in peace daily. Just like wearing a pair of shoes that are too tight or narrow for your feet can cause pain and damage, stress can cause a great deal of harm to your life.

What is Stress?

I used the analogy about shoes being too tight because the word stress comes from the Latin word, "strictus," which means tight or narrow, or "stringere," which means to tighten. Stress can be a result of physical and/or mental demands.

While stress has been around since the fall of man, stress theory research didn't begin until the 1920s or 30s by Hans Selye and Walter Cannon. Mr. Selye studied the stimulus/response (SR) processes. Walter Cannon studied the fight or flight responses in the human body. Both early researchers on the area of stress looked at the effects of good and bad stressors or pleasant and unpleasant.

Examples of pleasant stressors would be planning a wedding or preparing for a baby. Unpleasant stressors may include losing a job, dealing with a health problem, or having financial troubles. Good or bad stressors can be planned or unplanned as well.

Science of Stress:

When our bodies are stressed or stressors are perceived, our biological systems react by releasing hormones

Interview Shoes—Avoiding Dangerous Distractions

adrenaline and cortisol. God created our bodies to be able to do amazing things like handle stress. When I think of adrenaline, I think of a fun hormone that makes my body ready for action. Adrenaline makes your heart beat fast and your lungs breathe more efficiently. Your brain is more alert when this hormone kicks in, and you also have more energy as a result of the rise in sugar levels. However, it may also cause you to sweat, or as I like to say glisten.

Adrenaline also helps us to react to stressful situations by engaging our flight or fight response. When adrenaline is secreted, it helps us not to feel pain and to keep fighting or keeping going as needed. Adrenaline is also used in medications to alleviate allergic reactions, asthma, cardiac arrest, and others.

Cortisol is the main stress hormone. It helps your brain to repair tissues in the body. If your body is stressed, it manages the other systems in the body so your body can deal with the stress. It also helps you manage your mood, motivation, and fear.

Our stress hormones help our bodies react quickly to situations and can help us push through the impossible (such as in a race). The problem is that when these hormones are imbalanced, everything can get out of whack.

Our bodies weren't designed to stay in a stress state. Our stress hormones were created to do a job and return. Just like an EMT goes to an accident scene and then returns to their post, your hormones need to do their job and then return to restock. If we remain in a stressed-out state, our hormones can't balance. This can cause problems such as weight gain, anxiety, depression, headaches, muscle tension/pain, heart problems, and sleep issues. Cognitive impairment can occur. Not to mention, the social problems that can happen, such as frustrations in relationships, poor work performance, and children feeling neglected.[31]

Stress in America

Americans are among the most stressed people in the world. There are many reasons for this. Americans seem to have it all, so maybe the stress is related to the fear of losing what we have. We could debate it for sure, but there is no doubt we work more, rest and relax less, spend more, and eat more than in other countries. We also worry more about our children.[32]

There are many debatable reasons why Americans are more stressed compared to the rest of the world, but based on my personal observations I've noticed a few differences. One is schedules. Americans never stop to rest during the day and struggle to sleep at night. We also have more stuff, which leads us to have more to manage and take care of. Status and money are also higher on the American priority list than fostering healthy relationships with family and friends. We have much to learn from other cultures about managing stress and life, in general.

How Stress Affects People Differently

When I turned forty, I decided to go skydiving for the first time. I read a study that said skydiving instructors' stress levels were up the day before a jump, and a student's levels were lower the day before. On the other hand, on the day of the actual jump, the instructor's stress levels were lower, and the students were higher.[33]

Stress is dealt with differently by people. Have you ever noticed that some people don't get stressed about things that completely stress you out? It is also the same with managing stress. The same techniques don't work for every person. However, some things that can help us all manage stress properly.

Interview Shoes—Avoiding Dangerous Distractions

My Story of Stress

One of the ways I manage the stress of going to Walmart with my older sister on vacation is to have what I call "Walmart clothing adventures." She will not admit to this, but she takes FOREVER in Walmart. One time, while trying not to rush or get upset, I decided to take my mom and look at clothes. I got this amazing idea to try on ridiculous outfits. On one of our first adventures, I talked my mom (who, at that time, was in her mid-sixties) into trying on a bathing suit. It was a one-piece, or as we called them growing up, a "whole piece." The one-piece bathing suit was royal blue and had two eyes on the front, one of which was winking. It was hilarious to see my mom in this bathing suit. Not because she didn't look fantastic in it—watch out, Christie Brinkley—but because I'm sure the designer didn't have a sixty-something-year-old woman in mind at the time of design. This is one example of how we have fun in Walmart, which, at times, can be a stressful place. Over the years, many of my friends have also gotten in on the Walmart fun if we are on trips together. Try it the next time you feel stressed at Walmart!

At any rate, on another trip to Walmart with my sister, I found a great pair of red sandals for $5. They were so cute, and I got a ton of compliments on them, and no one believed they were from Walmart. Over the years, the soles of these shoes became worn out, so I decided to see if I could get the soles replaced. Yes, these shoes were that cute. It cost me $10 to replace the soles, but it was worth it.

We can replace the soles of shoes, but our bodies can't always overcome the stressors we allow or refuse to manage. I'm still working on everything written in this book, and I'm sure the messages from God are for me before anyone else. I have plenty of people in my life telling me I need to slow down; it is a constant balancing act and battle for me to find balance, but I'm not quitting, I'm working on it.

I CAN DO ANYTHING IN THE RIGHT PAIR OF SHOES

As I sit here and think, it is difficult for me to decide on the most stressful time in my life. Each phase of life has had various stressors. If you live long enough, you will likely have experienced grief, heartbreak, work problems, family concerns, health-related problems, trauma, frustrations, financial struggles, etc. The longer we live, the more stressors we will encounter. This world is full of trouble. But I have great news, Jesus came to give us peace! John 16:33 (NIV) says, "I have told you these things, so that in me you may have peace. In this world you will have trouble. But take heart! I have overcome the world." Jesus tells his followers because he knows they are discouraged and want to give up (John 16:1, NIV).
In Jesus' first message to his followers, He also says,

> *"So I tell you, don't worry about the food or drink you need to live, or about the clothes you need for your body. Life is more than food, and the body is more than clothes. Look at the birds in the air. They don't plant or harvest or store food in barns, but your heavenly Father feeds them. And you know that you are worth much more than the birds. You cannot add any time to your life by worrying about it. "And why do you worry about clothes? Look at how the lilies in the field grow. They don't work or make clothes for themselves. But I tell you that even Solomon with his riches was not dressed as beautifully as one of these flowers. God clothes the grass in the field, which is alive today but tomorrow is thrown into the fire. So you can be even more sure that God will clothe you. Don't have so little faith! Don't worry and say, 'What will we eat?' or 'What will we drink?' or 'What will we wear?' The people who don't know God keep trying to get these things, and your Father in heaven knows you need them.*

Interview Shoes—Avoiding Dangerous Distractions

Seek first God's kingdom and what God wants. Then all your other needs will be met as well. So don't worry about tomorrow, because tomorrow will have its own worries. Each day has enough trouble of its own."
Matthew 6:25-34, ESV

The conclusion I glean is that God wants us to remember and have faith that He will take care of us. He encourages us to remember by recounting His blessings, praying, and focusing our minds on Him. It takes daily practice and discipline, but it is the answer Jesus provides until He returns.

Matthew Henry's commentary on Matthew 6, says it this way: "The conclusion of the whole matter is, that it is the will and command of the Lord Jesus, that by daily prayers we may get strength to bear us up under our daily troubles, and to arm us against the temptations that attend them, and then let none of these things move us."[34]

Also, in Ephesians 6:15 (NLT), we are instructed to, "For shoes, put on the peace that comes from the Good News so that you will be fully prepared." To put on the shoes of peace and be prepared for anything the enemy throws our way in the area of stress, we must manage our stress.

Stress Management Strategies

1. **Define your problem**. You may need to seek the help of a professional such as a counselor to help with this. However, the first step in finding a solution to any problem is defining it well.

2. **Be positive**. Choose to have a good attitude in all circumstances.

3. **Focus on today**. Don't bring tomorrow's worries into today.

I CAN DO ANYTHING IN THE RIGHT PAIR OF SHOES

4. **Check your perspective**. Should I really get upset that I need to unload the dishwasher (among 1000 other things I need to do today), when unloading the dishwasher takes less than three minutes? I've timed myself.

5. **Process**, and talk about your stress with helpful people.

6. **Allow yourself to make mistakes** and decide to keep going.

7. **Surround yourself with supportive people** who will cheer you on but who will also tell you when you need to rest.

8. **Make a plan to grow** each year by setting personal, professional, spiritual, and other goals. This can help you keep your priorities in the right order, which will help you manage stress.

9. **Reflect on your stress management plan regularly**. Do you need to do more yoga or walking, eat less fried food, etc? Think about what is and isn't working to help you manage your stress.

10. **Exercise**: Yes; this helps everyone who is stressed. No, you don't need to be a crazy Crossfitter. Just go for a walk.

11. **Listen to your body**. Do you feel the need to rest, slow down, or pick up the pace?

12. **Take your thoughts captive**. Slow your thinking down by asking yourself questions like: Why is this stressful? Is it a new problem? Am I doing what I can to manage the stress? Also, redirect your thoughts. For example, if you see an accident, think of a good memory, and see how your body responds. This is one way to take your thoughts captive. Call one of your "go-tos" who can make you laugh.

13. **Blow off steam**: There is research that says screaming can release stress. Just saying. Go outside, and scream your head off. Do not scream at others!
14. **Have fun!**
15. **Do good:** Overcome evil by doing good. Pick up a hitchhiker, buy someone's groceries, etc.

Psalm 29:11, ESV
May the Lord give strength to his people!
May the Lord bless[a] his people with peace!

Peace Meditation

Close your eyes. Begin to think of peaceful images.

You are living in turbulent times. It may seem as if peace is impossible. However, as you begin to slow your breathing, think of peaceful images. Take a deep breath, hold it in for a few moments, and then push it all out. You may see an ocean, a mountain, a grassy field. Let your mind wander into the peaceful environment.

Take another deep breath. Think about the goodness of God. How has God been good to you? You have clothes, food, shelter, a church, family, and friends.

Keep breathing. Think about Jesus and how He is called the Prince of Peace. He made a way for us to have peace with God. Think about your unhindered access to and relationship with the God of the universe.

Take a deep breath, and think about the vastness of the universe and then how the Great Creator of all chose to have a relationship with you.

Now, think about Colossians 3:15, "And let the peace of Christ rule in your hearts, to which indeed you were called in one body. And be thankful." Consider how you can let the peace of Christ rule in your heart (mind, soul, spirit).

Think of the areas in which you need God's peace in your life. Be thankful that Christ can give you peace there.

Take a deep breath, and imagine what your life will look like as you allow the peace of Christ to rule in your heart. Now, ask God to give you this peace.

Take another deep breath, and thank God for his peace. Open your eyes . . . I can walk in peace by managing my stress.

Verses to meditate on if you are stressed:

Do not be anxious about anything, but in everything by prayer and supplication with thanksgiving let your requests be made known to God. And the peace of God, which transcends all understanding, will guard your hearts and your minds in Christ Jesus.
Philippians 4:6-7, ESV

Peace I leave with you; my peace I give to you. Not as the world gives do I give to you. Let not your hearts be troubled, neither let them be afraid.
John 14:27, ESV

Cast your burden on the Lord, and he will sustain you; he will never permit the righteous to be moved.
Psalm 55:22, ESV

Anxiety in a man's heart weighs him down, but a good word makes him glad.
Proverbs 12:25, ESV

Interview Shoes — Avoiding Dangerous Distractions

Out of my distress I called on the Lord; the Lord answered me and set me free. The Lord is on my side; I will not fear. What can man do to me?
Psalm 118:5-6, ESV

Blessed is the man who remains steadfast under trial, for when he has stood the test he will receive the crown of life, which God has promised to those who love him.
James 1:12, ESV

Therefore do not be anxious about tomorrow, for tomorrow will be anxious for itself. Sufficient for the day is its own trouble.
Matthew 6:34, ESV

And which of you by being anxious can add a single hour to his span of life?
Matthew 6:27, ESV

Casting all your anxieties on him, because he cares for you.
1 Peter 5:7 ESV

In peace I will lie down and sleep, for you alone, LORD, make me dwell in safety.
Psalm 4:8 ESV

Now may the Lord of peace himself give you peace at all times and in every way. The Lord be with all of you.
2 Thessalonians 3:16, ESV

Whatever you have learned or received or heard from me, or seen in me—put it into practice. And

I CAN DO ANYTHING IN THE RIGHT PAIR OF SHOES

the God of peace will be with you.
Philippians 4:9, ESV

*But the fruit of the Spirit is love, joy, peace,
forbearance, kindness, goodness, faithfulness…*
Galatians 5:22, ESV

*Let the peace of Christ rule in your hearts,
since as members of one body you were called
to peace. And be thankful.*
Colossians 3:15, ESV

*The mind governed by the flesh is death, but the
mind governed by the Spirit is life and peace.*
Romans 8:6, ESV

*You will keep in perfect peace those whose minds
are steadfast, because they trust in you.*
Isaiah 26:3, ESV

*The LORD gives strength to his people;
the LORD blesses his people with peace.*

**I will walk in peace by managing
the great distraction-stress!**

ELEVEN

Personalized—Stop Making Everything about Me

"Never enter the home of another with dust on your shoes and selfish expectations in your heart."
—Stewart Stafford, actor[35]

The focus today is very much on "self." Self-help, self-love, self-esteem, self-confidence, self-identity, choosing a pronoun for yourself, the list goes on. Selfishness, or narcissism at the extreme, is the plague of today. Tim Keller said in his book *The Freedom of Self-Forgetfulness*, "Up until the twentieth century, traditional cultures (and this is still true of most cultures in the world) always believed that too high a view of yourself was the root cause of all the evil in the world."[36] Jesus taught us, to put on peace, we must die to ourselves. Our lives, unlike our shoes, which are not harmed by a little personalization, should be less personalized and more focused on serving others.

I love a good monogrammed item, as much as the next mom, but when people start getting their Converse monogrammed, that is a bit much for me. It's not like you are going to lose them somewhere. My dad took it to another level: I found some of his old military travel bags that had his social security number stenciled onto them. He has since gotten rid of these, thankfully. We love our initials on everything, and I don't think this is because we don't want people to confuse our stuff with theirs.

There are a ton of athletes and celebrities who have shoes named after them. Most notable is the Air Jordan, created in 1984, in honor of famous basketball player, Michael Jordan. As the story goes, Adidas and Converse were the official shoes of the NBA, at the time, but neither of those shoe lines wanted to elevate Jordan above other players.[37] From a financial standpoint, I'm sure both companies have regretted the decision not to design a shoe for Jordan ever since. However, Con Jordan or Adidas Jordan just doesn't have the same ring.

Most of us cannot imagine having a shoe named after us. However, a simple Google search can show you how to design your own shoe or even how to start your own brand. The only thing custom-made about any shoe I own is the custom-made orthotics in my running shoes.

Interestingly, to me, the increase in focus on self has been on the same trajectory as the Air Jordan. Shoe companies then didn't want to elevate one above another, but now they do.

The terminology seems unending. There's self-centeredness, selfishness, self-love, self-esteem, self-confidence, self-worth, self-efficacy, self-reliance, self-awareness, self-actualization, self-care, self-respect, self-help, self-identity, self-talk, self-control, self-affirmation, self-regard, etc. It is kind of ridiculous. Not to mention the thousands of books written on self-esteem today. It seems as if Americans should have come to the conclusion that if we solve the "self-esteem problem," all will be right with the world.

However, I believe the reality is quite the opposite. In her 2002 New York Times article, *The Problem with Self-Esteem*, psychologist Lauren Slater wrote, "Self-esteem, as a construct, as a quasi religion, is woven into a tradition that both defines and confines us as Americans. If we were to deconstruct self-esteem, to question its value, we would be, in a sense, questioning who we are, nationally and individually. We would be threatening our self-esteem." [38] In this intriguing article, she asked great questions about self-esteem and the arguably misplaced value we've put on it today. She discussed how, after being assessed, serial killers, abusers, and other criminals don't actually suffer from low self-esteem. Isn't this interesting? But if you think about it, doesn't it make sense? If my husband beat me, obviously, he thought too highly of himself and too lowly of me.

Self-love, in its most extreme form, could be labeled narcissism. Narcissism is a term used to describe extreme self-centeredness to the extent that individuals ignore the thoughts, feelings, and needs of anyone around them. Narcissism is believed by some to be at the heart of every personality disorder. Narcissism and discussions surrounding the term are on the rise all over the U.S., from business and industry, to the church. At some level, we elevate individuals who, at first glance, seem to have it all together and seem to love themselves to the point of achieving great success as defined by the world (financial status, influence, beauty). It makes me wonder if our focus on self-esteem, or self in general, as a culture, has elevated and somewhat promoted narcissism even within the church, as scary as that may sound. However, all you have to do is listen to the podcast *The Rise and Fall of Mars Hill* to know that it is absolutely happening in the church, a place that should be defined by humility and sacrifice, not self-love and self-promotion.

What the Bible Says

Let's start at the very beginning of man: "Now the serpent was more crafty than any of the wild animals the LORD God had made . . . the serpent said to the woman, 'You will not surely die. For God knows that **when you eat of it your eyes** will be opened, and you will be like God, knowing good and evil'"** (Genesis 3:1-5, ESV, emphasis added).

First of all, the serpent (the Enemy) was thrown from heaven for pride.

> *You were blameless in your ways from the day you were created till wickedness was found in you. Through your widespread trade you were filled with violence, and you sinned. So I drove you in disgrace from the mount of God, and I expelled you, guardian cherub, from among the fiery stones. Your heart became proud on account of your beauty, and you corrupted your wisdom because of your splendor. So I threw you to the earth; I made a spectacle of you before kings. By your many sins and dishonest trade you have desecrated your sanctuaries. So I made a fire come out from you, and it consumed you, and I reduced you to ashes on the ground in the sight of all who were watching.*
> Ezekiel 28:15-18, NIV

Second of all, Adam and Eve made the choice to descern good and evil in their own eyes by eating from the forbidden tree. This led to a fal and curse the world still feeels today. Beyond Adam and Eve and the serpent were fallen beings who also rebelled against God (Genesis 6) creating a world of chaos. Finally, The Tower of Babel story in Genesis 11 is the ultimate picture of what happens when man and divine beings (Psalm 82) attempt to usurp God's authority, seeking to elevate themselves above the only One, Yahweh God, who is worthy to be above all. Murder, lying, cheating, sexual abuse, child exploitation, abandonment, financial struggles, physical ailments, and so on are all a result of these rebellions.

C.S. Lewis speaks for many Christian moralists when

Personalized—Stop Making Everything about Me

he calls pride "the essential vice, the utmost evil." He asserts that pride "is the complete anti-God state of mind." When discussing the topic of self-esteem, I realize some people also want to bring up the verse in Matthew 22:39 when Jesus says, "You shall love your neighbor as yourself," as an indication we *should* love ourselves. However, taking the entire word of God into account, this implies that we naturally already love ourselves, but we should actively love others, which isn't always natural.

Jesus didn't come to focus on Himself. He came to die for us. He served others. He healed others. He loved others. Don't you want to be known in the same manner?

C.S. Lewis said in *The Great Divorce*, " . . . what we called love is mostly the craving to be loved . . . You cannot love a fellow creature fully till you love God. We should love God because he is God not a means to an end . . . There is but one good, that is God. Everything else is good when it looks to Him and bad when it turns from Him."[39] Loving God and then loving yourself and others is how you can fully know love. It is not just about loving yourself.

The Bible teaches us to crucify our flesh. This is graphic, but basically, we should kill our selfish natures, or rather, let God transform them: "Those who belong to Christ Jesus have crucified the flesh with its passions and desires" (Galatians 5:24, ESV). In this verse, it's clear that crucifying the flesh is not something done *to* the believer but *by* the believer: "Those who belong to Christ have crucified the flesh."

Romans 6:6, ESV, says, "We know that our old self was crucified with him that the body of sin might be brought to nothing, so that we would no longer be enslaved to sin." This is quite the opposite of psychology's modern-day focus on self-everything! However, I truly believe it is the cure.

Christ showed us the beauty in serving others through many acts, but one of my favorites is when he washed the disciples' feet! My feet are jacked, and I regularly keep them groomed and my toenails painted so they look better. I can't imagine if they were calloused and dirty from walking around nasty roads during the days Jesus walked the earth. I love my husband, but he won't even massage my feet. His excuse is, "I don't do feet." To which I reply, "Crucify your flesh, and be like Jesus!"

Read it for Yourself

It was just before the Passover Festival. Jesus knew that the hour had come for him to leave this world and go to the Father. Having loved his own who were in the world, he loved them to the end. The evening meal was in progress, and the devil had already prompted Judas, the son of Simon Iscariot, to betray Jesus. Jesus knew that the Father had put all things under his power, and that he had come from God and was returning to God; so he got up from the meal, took off his outer clothing, and wrapped a towel around his waist. After that, he poured water into a basin and began to wash his disciples' feet, drying them with the towel that was wrapped around him. He came to Simon Peter, who said to him, "Lord, are you going to wash my feet?"
John 13:1-17, ESV

I want to encourage you to seek the word out and see how amazing it truly is!

I tried this with my grandmother before she passed away. I'm unsure what happens to our feet as we age, but they become pretty rough. Somehow, my grandmother convinced me to give her pedicures years before she went into a nursing home because she couldn't reach her toes. Her toenails could have stabbed and killed someone. I apologize Grandma (God rest her soul), but they didn't always smell nice either. Anyway, I did my best. My sisters tell me I will have to do Mom's too, to which I say, "Nope; I did Grandma's, so it is someone else's turn."

After the experience of washing the feet of my grandmother, let me just say, I *know* Jesus truly loved his disciples and set the most amazing example ever of servanthood. Servanthood isn't always sexy as the world wants us to believe, but it is what we are supposed to do as followers of Jesus. When you are serving others, you are doing what you were created to do, love others. Focusing on others versus yourself is a way to walk in peace because you are sharing love each time you serve others. If Jesus is your Lord and Savior, walking in peace is being prepared to share His love with others. If you are focused on yourself, you are not putting on the shoes of peace.

Scripture also says it is better to give than to receive. Acts 20:35, ESV: "In all things I have shown you that by working hard in this way we must help the weak and remember the words of the Lord Jesus, how he himself said, 'It is more blessed to give than to receive.'" While I'm not always convinced that it is better to give a pedicure than to receive one, I will continue to follow Jesus nonetheless. Seriously, the times I've been blessed to do good things for others have always made me feel better than the times when I'm just focused on myself. God's ways are truly higher and better than ours.

What should we do instead of focusing on "self"?

First, let me say what selflessness DOES NOT look like. It does not look like being a doormat, allowing others to abuse you, or not taking care of yourself. Nor does selflessness go to the opposite of self-love, which is self-hate. In my opinion, a better approach to viewing ourselves and seeking peace is self-appraisal.

Galatians 6:4 says, "Each one should test their own actions." Self-appraisal involves being honest about your strengths and weaknesses and being willing to evaluate and change as needed. The way I do this is to journal prayers about my strengths and weaknesses and ask God to help me. I must write in honesty, and my prayer journal is a safe place for me to do so. At times, I also ask my husband, family, or friends to be honest with me about my struggles. These conversations are not easy, but they are worth it, because I can grow, if I am receptive to feedback and learn from others speaking truth in love to me. This would be a great way to begin a process for another self-concept that Scripture talks about—self-control.

Self-control is part of the fruit of the spirit. We should ask the Holy Spirit each day to help us control ourselves and love others well.

For this very reason, make every effort to add to your faith goodness; and to goodness, knowledge; and to knowledge, self-control; and to self-control, perseverance; and to perseverance, godliness; and to godliness, mutual affection; and to mutual affection, love.
2 Peter 1:5-7, NIV

But the fruit of the Spirit is love, joy, peace, forbearance, kindness, goodness, faithfulness, gentleness and self-control. Against such things there is no law.
Galatians 5:22-23, NIV

If you are struggling to begin doing self-appraisal, below are some questions to get you started:

Daily Self-Appraisal:
1. In what areas did I think about myself too much today?

2. Did I serve others today? If so, how?
3. How did I control myself today?
4. How did I love others well today?

Contributions From Selfless People in History

Mother Teresa

Born Agnes Gonxha Bojaxhiu, she became a nun and was granted permission to provide food for the needy. Mother Teresa founded "The Missionaries of Charity," which began in India and would later grow to have branches in fifty Indian cities and thirty in other countries. A recipient of the Nobel Peace Prize, her philosophy of actively helping the poor in every way is by far her greatest humanitarian contribution.[40]

Martin Luther King, Jr.

He is known for his practice of non-violence as a protest against injustice. As a pastor in Alabama, he was one of the first to defend Rosa Parks. His role in the American Civil Rights Movement would later grow, and he would give the *I Have a Dream* speech that has inspired so many other humanitarians. Dr. King also received the Nobel Peace Prize.[41]

Ruth Bell Graham

As a young girl, in a small hospital compound, Ruth first sensed the great calling to abandon all for the sake of the Gospel of Jesus Christ. Her childhood was spent on China's mission field with her parents and siblings, surrounded by disease, despair, and the eventual disorder and chaos of civil wars. The suffering she observed only strengthened in her the conviction of mankind's need for the Savior..[42]

I CAN DO ANYTHING IN THE RIGHT PAIR OF SHOES

Verses to meditate on to combat selfishness and pride:

The LORD Almighty has a day in store for all the proud and lofty, for all that is exalted (and they will be humbled)...
Isaiah 2:12, NIV

But he gives us more grace. That is why Scripture says: "God opposes the proud but shows favor to the humble."
James 4:6, NIV

This is what the LORD says: "Let not the wise boast of their wisdom or the strong boast of their strength or the rich boast of their riches...
Jeremiah 9:23, NIV

Do nothing out of selfish ambition or vain conceit. Rather, in humility value others above yourselves...
Philippians 2:3, NIV

To fear the LORD is to hate evil; I hate pride and arrogance, evil behavior and perverse speech.
Proverbs 8:13, NIV

When pride comes, then comes disgrace, but with humility comes wisdom
Proverbs 11:2, NIV

The LORD detests all the proud of heart. Be sure of this: They will not go unpunished.
Proverbs 16:5, NIV

Pride goes before destruction, a haughty spirit before a fall.
Proverbs 16:18, NIV

Personalized—Stop Making Everything about Me

Before a downfall the heart is haughty, but humility comes before honor.
Proverbs 18:12, NIV

Haughty eyes and a proud heart— the unplowed field of the wicked—produce sin.
Proverbs 21:4, NIV

Do you see a person wise in their own eyes? There is more hope for a fool than for them.
Proverbs 26:12, NIV

Let someone else praise you, and not your own mouth; an outsider, and not your own lips.
Proverbs 27:2, NIV

Pride brings a person low, but the lowly in spirit gain honor.
Proverbs 29:23, NIV

In his pride the wicked man does not seek him; in all his thoughts there is no room for God.
Psalm 10:4, NIV

For by the grace given me I say to every one of you: Do not think of yourself more highly than you ought, but rather think of yourself with sober judgment, in accordance with the faith God has distributed to each of you.
Romans 12:3, NIV

Live in harmony with one another. Do not be proud, but be willing to associate with people of low position. Do not be conceited.
Romans 12:16, NIV

I CAN DO ANYTHING IN THE RIGHT PAIR OF SHOES

Love is patient, love is kind. It does not envy,
it does not boast, it is not proud.
1 Corinthians 13:4, NIV

Try reciting this daily as, what I call, a "Morning Mindset":
I will love others well today. I will put others first. Today, I will serve as Jesus did. I will think of others more than I think of myself. I will control myself and ask the Holy Spirit for help.

I will walk in peace by not making everything about myself.

Personalized—Stop Making Everything about Me

PART THREE

Finding Peace with Your Future

"There was this big black sole, and then, thank God, there was this girl painting her nails red at the time."
— Christian Louboutin, French fashion designer[43]

TWELVE

Red Soles—Developing a Healthy Outlook

I don't own a pair of Christian Louboutins, the very famous brand of shoes with red soles, but I find it interesting that the creator considered the sole as a part of the design to be noticed by others. After only two years of having a designer line of shoes, Louboutin thought his design was bland. When he looked over at an assistant who was painting her nails red, he had the idea to take the polish and paint the soles of the shoes. This simple change catapulted him into success, impacting everyone around him. Your perspective or outlook on life will impact your future and those around you in a positive or negative direction.

Maybe one small change, such as adding color to a product, has made you an extremely successful business person, but have you fallen in love with a pair of shoes that were just a little tight and needed one size up? I hate shoes that don't come in half sizes. A half of a size bigger or smaller could make the difference between a blister or a comfortable walk. Similarly, even a small shift in our outlook or perspective can be life-changing and can lead us to successfully walk in peace. Changing your outlook each day requires work and intentionality, no matter how small the shift may be, but that change may impact everyone around you.

Have you ever worn a pair of shoes, and that one decision impacted everyone around you? Or, have you ever not had the appropriate shoes for a particular situation? In 2022, I went to Kenya with an anti-sex trafficking agency. While we were there, we went to meet with high-level government leaders to discuss matters related to our organization. I was not prepared with the appropriate attire, including shoes, for this meeting. We were required to wear professional dress attire. If I had prepared for this event, I could have saved money, time, and energy.

Planning my shoes for the day, or an event, is important for me to feel peaceful. More importantly, choosing to develop a healthy outlook, by preparing my mind each morning to have a positive perspective for the day, is a strategy I use to walk in peace. I wish I could tell you that every morning of my life, I'd intentionally planned to have a healthy outlook and perspective for the day. If I consider the shoes I wear each day, based on weather, cultural situations, and length of time wearing them, I should probably spend more time preparing my mind. Think of the difference it could make.

Unfortunately, we don't stop to consider what influences our perspective. We react to things, situations, or people. To walk in peace in the future, we must be aware of where our perspectives and outlooks come from, what they are influenced by, and who they potentially impact.

Perspective and Its Impact on Others

A couple of years ago, I went on a girl's trip to Chicago. My friend, Candice, is a famous DJ, and she took me and some other friends on a trip, where she was the DJ for a convention with the actors and actresses from "Chicago Fire", "Chicago Med", and "Chicago PD". At one of the evening events, one of my friends and I took a break and went outside for some air. Outside, we met a real Chicago fireman who was also attending the event. We ended up having a great conversation with him and some others about parenting. However, while talking about having teenagers, I jokingly told him I wanted "Chloe the Hoe-y" to stay away from my son.

There was no Chloe in my son's life at the time; I just used the name as a play on words. Sadly, I didn't stop to consider the possibility that the fireman's daughter's name was Chloe. When he said, "Oh, my daughter's name is Chloe," I about fell out. Talk about sticking your foot in your mouth and not feeling peaceful in the moment! A little forethought could have helped me here. I should have considered the possibility that the fireman had a daughter named Chloe or that anyone named Chloe may not appreciate me using this name this way. My outlook on joking around with others has changed. I must consider what the other person is thinking or consider how he or she is feeling about what I am saying to walk in peace.

In preparing and planning to walk in peace each day, we should always be considerate of others before we open our mouths. We live in a world full of controversial names, differing cultures, vast opinions, hostile political climates, choice of pronouns, etc. We could easily get stuck in our own silos, falsely thinking we are always right about everything. Our goal in developing a healthy outlook that leads to walking in peace in a turbulent world should be to bridge the gap of our differences, at times, and develop healthy relationships by having productive conversations.

While having productive conversations, we cannot hide away in groups of those who only believe what we believe, look like we do, and like what we like. There are beautiful people all around us in need of a Savior. We need to put on the shoes of peace by adjusting our perspective and allowing ourselves to see the beauty and potential of others. This doesn't mean we change the truth of the gospel; it means we need to consider where others are coming from and show them we care, if we expect them to ever want to hear the truth.

Having productive conversations should also include your communication behaviors on social media. In the social media-crazed world we live in, we've been taught to react to things by liking, disliking, sending emojis, etc. Have you ever stopped and considered why you are sending a specific emoji? Or, do you consider what perspective those following you may have about a specific issue? I often cringe at things people post, thinking about the wide range of the potential audience. Most people don't realize that what they "like" on social media is leading them to a place of bias and not peace.

Bias often torments our world; therefore, journeying in peace involves not only being aware of your own perspective but also being respectful of the perspective of others by realizing their outlook is different. You may see the beautiful Louboutin red sole on a shoe, while someone else may see only the high heel. Wearing a shoe gives you a different perspective than observing a shoe on someone else. When you put on peace, remember to be prayerful and considerate of those who are different than you. I had to be considerate of the culture I was in while choosing shoes for an important meeting because how I dressed was a sign of respect to those I was around. Consider others' souls and how your actions impact them.

Consider Your Biases

Have you heard of the term confirmation bias? Oxford Languages defines it as the tendency to interpret new evidence as confirmation of one's existing beliefs or theories.[44] Confirmation bias happens when you are processing information, but there is a systematic error in your thinking. The error in your thinking leads you to accept only new information that confirms what you already believe and causes you to tune out anything that contradicts what you believe. If we never consider the perspectives of others or love them by listening, we are preventing our roots from growing deeper in our faith.

Here are some ways you may be a victim of confirmation bias and aren't aware:

- Misinterpreting or manipulating information to fit your beliefs
- Searching online for evidence that backs up your existing beliefs
- Trying to make others believe what you believe
- Neglecting any contradictory information
- Desiring to associate with only those who have your same beliefs
- Believing others whose beliefs don't align with yours have ulterior motives

Confirmation bias can be dangerous. People come into my office frequently stating they have diagnosed themselves with a specific mental health disorder after "researching" it. When we search for certain things on the internet, algorithms are designed to send us more of what we are seeking or searching. In the same way, when you like a post or view something on social media, you will soon notice more of what you "liked." Thanks to algorithms, we are fed the same things over and over, which can build bias in our minds.

Consider the danger in the political divide of our nation, the racial divide of our nation, and varying religious views and divisions. If we never do a second Google search, ask more questions, or follow those who are different than us, we will fall prey to the enemy's strategy of using confirmation bias against us. This, in turn, prevents us from seeking peace in our communities.

So, how do we avoid bias? First of all, it is important to be aware of them. Consider where your perspective comes from. We are influenced by our family, friends, environment, faith, etc. Consider what it would be like if you were someone else, from somewhere else, of a different faith. How does our perspective influence our actions, attitudes, and behaviors?

Consider how teams prepare to meet their arch-rivals. They watch films and study their opponents. Just like a good attorney has to consider what their opponent is going to say to defend their position, shouldn't we also consider the differing perspectives of others to better understand and defend our own? Of course, this is not the only reason. By looking at other viewpoints, we can learn why some people believe the way they do or how they are defining their values, and in turn, learn to be more compassionate and have empathy towards those who are different than us. It is a blessing and joy to be able to talk about differences instead of fighting over them.

Consider Others

One of my neighbors is from a different cultural background than most in my neighborhood. Her family is from India. Several years ago, I told her I was going on a trip to her hometown, Ahmedabad, India, and she was excited and shocked. Not many people from the US travel to India, especially to her hometown of Ahmedabad. Sadly, many immigrants think those who were born in America have no desire to learn or understand different cultures. Let's be honest, sometimes we don't.

To prepare for the trip, a group from my church at the time studied and prepared to travel to India. We learned about the different religions by reading and discussing different topics for weeks. Our leader, at the time, would lay out different books each week for us to read, and we all tried to fight over the shorter books. One week, I got the biggest book, and it turned out to be my favorite. It was *Seeking Allah, Finding Jesus* by Nabeel Qureshi. I highly recommend it!

Another one of our strategies for preparation was to meet with Indians we knew living in our area. The population of Indians in the area where I live has drastically increased over the years. I can't thank God enough for allowing my friend, Rekha, to live near me. I met with her as I prepared for the trip, and God has blessed me with her friendship.

Arguably, Rekha's perspective of me changed when I told her I was going to India, as did mine after meeting with her and learning from her by asking questions. Her family allowed me into their home, cooked for me and my family (because my paneer turned out poorly), and invited us to events related to their culture. It was a beautiful thing!

Over lunch one day, God allowed me to share my faith in Jesus with Rehka, as she shared her Hindu faith with me. I would never have been able to share my faith with her had I not opened myself up to also listening about hers. Relationships are key to truly making a difference in the lives of others. Jesus offers us a relationship with God. He is not some far-away power in the universe who is impersonal and just gives out rules. He is a loving God who wants to be our father. He wants to be near us and with us, and if we seek to have relationships with others, then we can share the gospel of peace with them.

Consider Your Actions

While we were surprised by some things on the trip, we did prepare to have good attitudes, as we were going to work and serve others. Choosing to have a good attitude was helpful; especially when we encountered unexpected situations, such as a kid watching the movie *Peter Rabbit* fifteen times and yelling loudly at his screen each time on our thirteen-hour flight. Remaining positively silly helped me when seeing someone in our group with toilet paper sticking out of his pants as we disembarked from the airplane and also when receiving computer paper at our "hotel" when we asked for toilet paper.

When we arrived in India, the van that picked us up from the airport was complete with curtains and a ladder leading to the top of the van. In America, curtains on a van are a red flag. However, we didn't have a choice; we had to get in the van. You can't possibly prepare for everything, but again, choosing to have a good attitude, and in this case, an adventurous spirit, is something you *can* prepare for. As we got in the culturally appropriate van, I chose to make it a teachable moment for the younger volunteers on the trip. I chose to joke with them and also suggested that while appropriate in India, when we returned home, it was not advisable to get into a van with curtains. I'm sure this lesson had a profound impact on their lives.

Actually, I know that it did because they changed their perspectives toward me as some unrelatable, uptight, older woman and became my friends on the trip. I've even become their godmother. This was an unexpected blessing we didn't prepare for. Not only did we have cultural differences with those we went to serve, but we also had differences within the volunteer group. Their actions greatly impacted me! They embraced me, and we had a blast. Fast forward a couple of years, and they still text, call, and Snapchat me, all because we chose to walk in peace by embracing our differences.

While in India, we were keenly aware of our differences and how our actions impacted others. Some of our differences included following cultural practices to be allowed entrance into certain places. One of these places was a 400+-year-old mosque. Studying the differences between Christianity and Islam before proved beneficial in terms of knowing how to behave, how to interact with others within the mosque, etc. For example, in this mosque, women were allowed but only in certain areas. We also had to take off our shoes in designated places.

Walking around a mosque barefoot was not something we were used to, and our feet became rather dirty, as the area had been in a drought and it was very dusty. Overall, our visit was well worth the time spent, as we were able to share the gospel with the Iman at the mosque and a group of Muslims. Sharing the gospel of Jesus with an Imam and Muslim followers was no easy task, and I'm pretty sure it wouldn't have been possible if we hadn't listened to them first. This is another example of how listening to others' perspectives and outlooks makes them more willing to listen to ours. We must show we care before others will ever care what we have to say. Putting on the shoes of peace that day required us to be respectful, understand another culture, and learn about another religion and different viewpoints.

As we left the mosque, we put our shoes back on to prepare to walk on the dirt road to our car. My feet were really dirty, so my friend and I decided to step in a puddle with my Birkenstock sandals on to attempt to clean my feet. Soon after, we noticed our feet started to smell terrible. Then as we began to take wet wipes and clean our feet and shoes, we saw a dog poop in the puddle. We discovered that this was, most likely, a frequent site for bathroom breaks for animals. It was hilarious and gross. Yet another lesson learned: *Never wash your feet in a puddle.*

The bottom line is, our actions matter and influence the perspective and outlook of others. As believers in Jesus Christ, our actions either lead others to Him or away from Him. Just like the smell of my stinky shoes impacted everyone around me, so do our actions. If we want to walk in peace, we must be people of the Word, those who are slow to speak and quick to listen, as stated in James 1:19. We must be people who overlook offenses (Proverbs 19:11), and we have to do everything in love (1 Corinthians 16:14).

The Misunderstanding of Jeremiah 29:11

Many people will never travel to a foreign country, but living in the USA, you don't have to go very far to meet people who are different from you. Unfortunately, many Christians today want to stay in their own circles of people with those who only believe what they believe. We have to be careful who we spend most of our time with, but we should never separate ourselves so much that we don't meet people who are different than us. We are called to be set apart, but that doesn't necessarily mean separating all of the time. I believe a great example of this is in the book of Jeremiah in chapter 29.

Jeremiah is writing to a group of Hebrews who were taken captive and living in exile in Babylon. The people were part of a group of exiles living in a city they didn't choose. Have you ever been sent to a place, job, or are you in a family you wouldn't have necessarily chosen?

Jeremiah, speaking as the Lord's prophet, instructs the people to build houses, plant gardens, and eat the fruit of the community they live in. He also says to marry and have children while living in exile. Jeremiah then tells them to:

> *". . . seek the peace of the city where I have caused you to be carried away captive, and pray to the LORD for it; for in its peace you will have peace."*
> Jeremiah 29:5-10, KJV

Do you see what I see in this passage? God tells them

to build houses, live, marry, and seek peace; He wants us to seek peace where we are. He never asked them to hide away and never interact with the Babylonians. Do you know people who only want to be around those who are just like them? God wanted the peace He gave His children to spread to those who weren't in His family.

Of course, He does warn the people not to be deceived by the teachings and ways of the Babylonians. We are to use discernment in all interactions and not be led away from the truth of the gospel. Putting on the shoes of peace requires us to be rooted in the Word. Like the Roman shoes had spikes in them to help them stand firm while facing the enemy, we should stand firm on the word of God as we engage in conversations with those who believe differently than us, which was especially helpful to me in India when in a mosque talking to an Imam about the gospel!

After the Lord tells them to seek peace, in verses 10–14, He says He will visit them after captivity and perform good work for them. He reminds them He has thoughts of peace and not evil to give them a hope and future! God asks them to have faith in believing He will bring them back from captivity.

As we put on the metaphorical shoes of peace, we are also making ourselves available to share the gospel with others in our conversations, especially in our responses. To respond to others, we have to engage in relationships with others who aren't necessarily believers in Jesus. We can't be passive, scared, cliquey, or fearful of those who are different. You can and should challenge yourself regularly to engage with those who aren't like you. If you are intimidated by different cultures around you or people who don't look like you, ask God to help you face this fear. You don't have to travel like I did to learn about others. It may only require that you walk next door. Have you done this lately? If not, how can you plan to in the near future?

This is also something, as parents, we should encourage our children to do, without fearing that they will be swayed from the values and beliefs we are teaching them. As a child, I asked a million questions. As I grew older, while working out my salvation and seeking to understand the things of God, I would ask my dad questions about different faiths. He was never frightened by me asking about Islam, Mormon, or different denominations. He even had some of the different religious texts. What I discovered about my dad is that he had an unwavering faith, believing that the truth would set me free in the end, and it did. God's word and truth are powerful; never doubt this in raising your kids. Live in a spirit of power and might, not fear.

My parents, allowing me to be around different cultures and allowing me to be inquisitive about different faiths, religions, etc., has allowed God to grow my roots deeper. God's Word says in Matthew 7:7, ESV, "Ask and it will be given to you; seek and you will find; knock and the door will be opened to you." Do we have that same unwavering faith today?

Sadly, I see too many parents today not allowing their children to ask questions. Maybe it's because we don't know the answers. Or, maybe it's because we are afraid that if they ask, they must be questioning the faith and will eventually leave it. At some point, we have to allow and even teach them to ask, so their roots can grow deeper and so we can encourage them to share the gospel with others.

Plan to Walk in Peace in the Future

Consider your biases, and build awareness by:

- Thinking about the things you see online that annoy you,
- Writing out your political, religious, and other views.

- Discussing reasons someone might believe something different than you.
- Following people on social media who disagree with you, along with people who align with your beliefs.

Consider others:

- Make it a practice to meet with someone different than you regularly.
- Add to your friend group regularly. Change it up.
- Learn about another culture, religion, or political mindset.
- Get to know your neighbors.
- Allow others, your kids, or family members to ask questions.
- Allow the differences of others to challenge instead of threaten you.

Consider your actions:

- Be slow to speak and quick to listen. (James 1:19)
- Listen actively (Consider your body language and nonverbal cues, don't interrupt, try not to judge, don't impose your thoughts and opinions unless asked, and ask questions). (Proverbs 2:2)
- Overlook offenses. Sensible people control their temper; they earn respect by overlooking wrongs. (Proverbs 19:11)
- Do everything in love. (1 Corinthians 16:14)

I CAN DO ANYTHING IN THE RIGHT PAIR OF SHOES

Now, write out your plan to consider your biases, consider others' perspectives, and consider how to respond to others in love.

My prayer for you to prepare to walk in peace in the future is for you to consider your biases, consider others, and consider your actions. Our world needs these kinds of people—characterized by what we are for, not what we are against; people who love at all costs. People who boldly proclaim the gospel of Jesus, by drawing people to His love for them, is what the world truly needs. May this be our outlook—realize people all around us are in need of a Savior.

Verses to meditate on as you prepare to embrace people who are different:

For I know the thoughts that I think toward you," says the LORD, "thoughts of peace and not of evil, to give you a future and a hope.
Jeremiah 29:11, NIV

My dear brothers and sisters, take note of this: Everyone should be quick to listen, slow to speak and slow to become angry
James 1:19, NIV

...turning your ear to wisdom and applying your heart to understanding
Proverbs 2:2, NIV

A person's wisdom yields patience; it is to one's glory to overlook an offense.
Proverbs 19:11

Be on your guard; stand firm in the faith; be courageous; be strong. Do everything in love.
1 Corinthians 16: 13-14, NIV

Love your neighbor as yourself.
Mark 12:31

I will walk in peace by having a healthy and loving outlook toward life and others!

THIRTEEN

The Collector's Item—Looking for Lessons Along the Way

You have big shoes to fill.

"I have too many shoes: said no woman ever."
—Source Unknown

A trendy (at the time of writing this book) part-time job of many young adults is buying, selling, and collecting high-end athletic sneakers online. It is a very intriguing trade. Sneakers began to rise in popularity when Michael Jordan and Nike partnered to make the Air Jordan brand.[45] Since that time, sneakers have become something people desire, collect, and sell. With the rise of online shopping, selling, trading, etc., many platforms are available for those wanting to invest in sneakers. It seemed silly to me, at first, but now I listen to my sons and their friends talk about what shoes "dropped" recently, and where to find them. You may not collect sneakers, but there is likely something you enjoy as much.

My son loves expensive sneakers and watching new ones "drop" on certain websites and shoe trading platforms. Some of the shoes are priced in the thousands. These shoes are valuable to some. The funny thing is, the expensive shoes my son has saved his money for and purchased are often the ones he rarely wears. Many collectors of you-name-it (coins, shoes,

I CAN DO ANYTHING IN THE RIGHT PAIR OF SHOES

antiques, etc.), would agree they may not even take certain items out of the packages due to their value.

People collect things for different reasons. Some believe collecting is a natural instinct humans developed over time. Today, many collect as a hobby because it brings joy, pleasure, or connection to a favorite pastime or sporting team. Serious collectors spend a lot of time and money investing in their collections. There is nothing wrong with collecting things, per se, but something more valuable than things is wisdom. Have you ever considered wisdom as something you can collect?

Let me encourage you to start a new collection, one you should value and treat delicately as one of your most prized possessions, but also, one you should use daily! Collecting wisdom is defined by learning from others who've paved the way for us in life. Of course, we can and should collect the lessons we've learned through our own experiences too. Learning and planning to walk in peace should involve collecting wisdom daily so we can have it for the future.

Can you imagine how well our days could go if we carefully considered choosing, *with wisdom*, words or lessons based on situations we find ourselves in? Conversely, our days can end up poorly if we don't choose the right shoes. Have you ever worn heels instead of rain boots in the rain or flip-flops on a hiking trail?

One time, I wore white canvas flip-flops to see the Statue of Liberty, then stepped into a sewage drain hole. Those flip-flops were a terrible choice for walking around New York City. Oh, how I wished I had worn tennis shoes.

Beyond choosing the right shoes for the right events, collecting wisdom to know what shoe to wear at the right time is important too. When I started running, I didn't lean on my own understanding (which was very minimal) about what shoes or even what socks to wear, for that matter. I asked people who had learned the lessons before I did, people who studied and sold running shoes for a living, and individuals who had been running a lot longer than I had been.

These days, with the ability to buy anything with the tap of a finger, "research," or find seemingly unending amounts of information on the Internet, we can be tempted to neglect the value of collecting wisdom from people we know. These days, people will consult Dr. WebMD or Dr. Healthline over their own medically-trained physician. I can't tell you how many times I've had clients come in having already determined their diagnosis. Let me interject a warning very quickly on this matter . . . DO NOT diagnose yourself. Don't go into a professional's office thinking you know more than he/she does because you looked it up online.

If I came to your place of work and acted like I knew everything based on my Internet search knowledge, you'd likely think I was crazy. There is a reason educational programs are accredited, and it takes a long time to earn a degree. Internet searches cannot supplant professional training.

God gave us so many words of wisdom in Scripture. He encouraged us to meditate on Scripture, learn from it, and seek His wisdom, which is not of this world. One way God has helped and is helping me to gain wisdom is by sending people into my life I can learn from. I value the things I've learned from people, as if the lessons are collector's items.

Wisdom from my Personal Collection

My family has taught me about everything from how to dress, how to be treated as a wife, how to treat siblings, how to love friends and others, how to manage finances, and how to be happy for others.

Here are just a few nuggets of wisdom:

I CAN DO ANYTHING IN THE RIGHT PAIR OF SHOES

Dad: He taught me to love God, first and foremost. He showed me how a woman should be loved by how he loves my mom. He taught me to serve those whom others may not want to love, such as prisoners or those in nursing homes. Dad showed me not to be fearful of people who believed differently than I believe. He taught me it was okay to question things and seek God on my own. **Biggest nugget: Love God with all your heart, mind, and soul.**

Mom: She taught me to dress for all occasions. She taught me how to let my beauty show from the inside out. She taught me to suck it up, keep going, and never quit. She has shown me how to parent my sons well when they are adults. She's an easy mother-in-law; she doesn't put any pressure on us to call her every day. She doesn't take people on guilt trips. She lets me figure things out. She has taught me to always make things right with my sisters. **Biggest nugget: Love others well by treating everyone as you want to be treated.**

My sisters: They love me at my worst and my best. My older sister has also taught me a lot about cooking, while my younger sister teaches me about fashion and style. We've grown up together, lived together, and are now raising children alongside one another. **Biggest nugget: Love unconditionally, regardless of your flaws.**

Extended family and godparents: My aunts, uncles, and godparents taught me to love children like they are the most important people in the room. Give them adventure. Celebrate what they are learning. Encourage them. Show up for them. Be proud of them. **Biggest nugget: Celebrate children, and realize they are the next generation of leaders!**

Husband: He teaches me things all the time, but I'll

The Collector's Item—Looking for Lessons Along the Way

never forget one of the first lessons he taught me, which was that no one cares as much about the way my feet and legs look as I do. I told him about my feet/legs, and he said, "So what? I get the best of both worlds, a little one and a big one!" and this was the moment I knew I'd make him marry me. **Biggest nugget: You are beautiful just the way you are.**

Neighbors: It's okay to be different. Let others help you. Learn new cultures. Get over your frustrations. Let people in; give people a chance. **Biggest nugget: Get outside of your comfort zone and get to know those who live near you!**

Youth Leaders: Laugh, have fun, and don't despise teenagers. Appreciate and support them throughout their lives. Serving God is serving others. Don't take life too seriously. **Biggest nugget: The main goal of life should be to love God and love others.**

Teachers: Learning should be fun. Keep trying. Don't give up. You can do more than you think you are capable of. Mistakes are a part of the process. **Biggest nugget: Be a life-long learner.**

Co-workers: Work hard, and be a good teammate. Work is not who you are. No matter what your career is, God loves that you are serving, and you can be amazing at anything. God doesn't care whether you are a maid or a doctor. **Biggest nugget: People have different talents and abilities, and they all can be used for God.**

Friends: Young friends teach you to laugh at yourself. Friends your age teach you that you aren't alone in this world to do the hard things, like raising kids. Friends from older generations teach you to enjoy each day and live life to its fullest.

I CAN DO ANYTHING IN THE RIGHT PAIR OF SHOES

Biggest nugget: You are not alone.

Pastors: They are sinners just like you are. The only person who belongs on some pedestal is God! We can all benefit from having a shepherd to lead us and teach us the things of God. **Biggest nugget: Be open to learning from those whom God has called to lead.**

Adopted Family or Framily: I'm not referring to legal adoption; although, that is awesome too. If you don't have a brother or sister, adopt one. If you need a dad, find someone who will be a father figure to you. I love my adopted family. I collect family members like lessons on wisdom! **Biggest Nugget: If you pray and ask God to send you relationships where you are lacking, He will!**

Clients: People can heal from hurts no matter how deep they are. There are amazing people in the world who've dealt with some crazy hurts. If I can be faithful for a small amount of time here on earth, all of eternity will be worth it. Love others well, even if they don't love you back. **Biggest nugget: People are capable of amazing things.**

Church People: There is a family you can choose. God sets the lonely in families. While some of my greatest hurts have come from church people, so has my greatest healing. **Biggest nugget: People are worth the risk, no matter how broken they are.**

One of a Kind

If you knew Maria, you'd know she deserves her own category. She would think it was hilarious that I compared her to a one of a kind shoe! I was privileged to work with her at one

The Collector's Item—Looking for Lessons Along the Way

of my first professional jobs out of college. She was a counselor at a VA hospital but also worked part-time at the community college where I worked. Some would say she wasn't a very attractive lady, according to the world's standards, but her personality and how she loved others was magnetic. I could probably write an entire book on just the way she loved others and how much it taught me to do the same. I truly believe she was one of the most beautiful examples of the love of Jesus.

Let me describe Maria a bit more for you. She was a white lady who went to a predominately black seminary and also called herself a part of a "frozen chosen" (her words not mine) church denomination. Maria truly loved everyone. Her choice to go to a different seminary than what most like her would choose was in an effort to learn from those who were different, and she also loved the black church.

Over the years (I knew her in her 50s and 60s), I watched Maria love so many different people. She had students ranging from preppy to scary-looking flock to her office. If you sat with her, you might hear her tell stories of being threatened by Veterans with PTSD she counseled, who turned into stories of breakthrough because she never gave up on them. The county jail had her number on speed dial because when someone was getting out of jail and had nowhere to go, they knew they could call Maria, and she would take them in. No matter how many people stole from her, she never stopped allowing people in her home. In fact, at the time of her death, one of her sons said there were twenty-seven keys to her house out and about because she had given so many to those who needed a place to stay. Maria made everyone feel like the most important person in the room and was one of the funniest people you'd ever met.

At her funeral, it was the most diverse group of people I'd ever seen at a funeral. We came from all walks of life, ethnicities, generations, etc. The wisdom Maria shared was based on the love she had for every soul she met. She was a rare gem, one we should all aspire to be like because she was like Jesus. The wisdom to collect from Maria was endless but was all centered in walking in peace by deeply loving and embracing others regardless of any difference that might exist. Maria's wisdom was like the collector's shoe that you would NEVER sell. She loved like Jesus did by laying down her life in the ways God called her to to love and serve others. **Biggest nugget: People are worthy of love no matter how far gone you think they are. Just love others, period, which is exactly what Jesus did.**

Biblical Application

I can't write a chapter on collecting wisdom without mentioning Solomon, the wisest man who ever lived. Solomon is also remembered as the most wealthy man who ever lived; still his legacy is in his wisdom. The biggest lesson I take from Solomon is to ask God for it. When you are planning to walk in peace and seeking to collect wisdom from others, the first step must be to ask God for wisdom. He will send people, experiences, and things your way to help you build your collection.

The Lord was pleased that Solomon had asked this. So God said to him, "You did not ask for a long life, or riches for yourself, or the death of your enemies. Since you asked for wisdom to make the right decisions, I will do what you asked. I will give you wisdom and understanding that is greater than anyone has had in the past or will have in the future. I will also give you what you did not ask for: riches and honor. During your life no other king will be as great as you. If you follow me and obey my laws and commands, as your father David did, I will also give you a long life."
1 Kings 3:13-15, ESV

The Collector's Item—Looking for Lessons Along the Way

Brief Tips to seek wisdom daily

- Read Proverbs every day. There is so much to contemplate and use daily.
- Journal lessons you learn. Write down what you've learned in the past, what you are learning daily, and what you'd like to learn. Then, review these often.
- Give people a chance: We can grow in wisdom by giving others a chance to teach us something.
- Take time to learn from others: Time is a hot commodity and one that is worth using to invest in learning from others.
- Treat lessons learned as valuable collectors' items: Make your wisdom journal a valued possession.
- Be a wise leader and good example.

Take time to journal some of the lessons you've learned from others here:

I CAN DO ANYTHING IN THE RIGHT PAIR OF SHOES

A Few Verses About Wisdom to Meditate on

If any of you lacks wisdom, let him ask God, who gives generously to all without reproach, and it will be given him.
James 1:5, ESV

But the wisdom from above is first pure, then peaceable, gentle, open to reason, full of mercy and good fruits, impartial and sincere.
James 3:17, ESV

Blessed is the one who finds wisdom, and the one who gets understanding, for the gain from her is better than gain from silver and her profit better than gold. She is more precious than jewels, and nothing you desire can compare with her. Long life is in her right hand; in her left hand are riches and honor. Her ways are ways of pleasantness, and all her paths are peace. ...
Proverbs 3:13-18, ESV

Look carefully then how you walk, not as unwise but as wise, making the best use of the time, because the days are evil. Therefore do not be foolish, but understand what the will of the Lord is.
Ephesians 5:15-17, ESV

Listen to advice and accept instruction, that you may gain wisdom in the future.
Proverbs 19:20, ESV

The way of a fool is right in his own eyes, but a wise man listens to advice
Proverbs 12:15, ESV

The Collector's Item—Looking for Lessons Along the Way

*Doing wrong is like a joke to a fool, but
wisdom is pleasure to a man of understanding.*
Proverbs 10:23, ESV

*Let the word of Christ dwell in you richly,
teaching and admonishing one another in all wisdom,
singing psalms and hymns and spiritual songs, with
thankfulness in your hearts to God.*
Colossians 3:16, ESV

*An intelligent heart acquires knowledge, and
the ear of the wise seeks knowledge.*
Proverbs 18:15, ESV

*For the Lord gives wisdom; from his mouth
come knowledge and understanding...*
Proverbs 2:6, ESV

*The fear of the Lord is the beginning of wisdom;
all those who practice it have a good understanding.
His praise endures forever!*
Psalm 111:10, ESV

*Whoever restrains his words has knowledge, and
he who has a cool spirit is a man of understanding.
Even a fool who keeps silent is considered wise;
when he closes his lips, he is deemed intelligent.*
Proverbs 17:27-28, ESV

*How much better to get wisdom than gold! To get
understanding is to be chosen rather than silver.*
Proverbs 16:16, ESV

For I will give you a mouth and wisdom, which

I CAN DO ANYTHING IN THE RIGHT PAIR OF SHOES

*none of your adversaries will be able to
withstand or contradict.*
Luke 21:15, ESV

*Be not wise in your own eyes; fear the Lord,
and turn away from evil.*
Proverbs 3:7, ESV

*The fear of the Lord is the beginning of wisdom,
and the knowledge of the Holy One is insight.*
Proverbs 9:10, ESV

*So teach us to number our days that we may
get a heart of wisdom.*
Psalm 90:12, ESV

*Do not forsake her, and she will keep you; love her,
and she will guard you. The beginning of wisdom is
this: Get wisdom, and whatever you get, get insight.*
Proverbs 4:6-7, ESV

*Who is wise and understanding among you? By
his good conduct let him show his works in
the meekness of wisdom.*
James 3:13, ESV

*For the protection of wisdom is like the protection
of money, and the advantage of knowledge is
that wisdom preserves the life of him who has it.*
Ecclesiastes 7:12, ESV

*The fear of the Lord is instruction in wisdom,
and humility comes before honor.*
Proverbs 15:33, ESV

The Collector's Item—Looking for Lessons Along the Way

*The wisdom of the prudent is to discern his way,
but the folly of fools is deceiving.*
Proverbs 14:8, ESV

*I do not cease to give thanks for you, remembering
you in my prayers, that the God of our Lord Jesus
Christ, the Father of glory, may give you a spirit of
wisdom and of revelation in the knowledge of him,
having the eyes of your hearts enlightened, that
you may know what is the hope to which he has
called you, what are the riches of his glorious
inheritance in the saints, and what is the
immeasurable greatness of his power toward
us who believe, according to the
working of his great might,*
Ephesians 1:16-19, ESV

*Wisdom is with the aged, and understanding in
length of days. "With God are wisdom and might;
he has counsel and understanding.*
Job 12:12-13, ESV

*Everyone then who hears these words of mine
and does them will be like a wise man who
built his house on the rock.*
Matthew 7:24, ESV

*By wisdom a house is built, and by understanding
it is established; by knowledge the rooms are
filled with all precious and pleasant riches. A wise
man is full of strength, and a man of knowledge
enhances his might, for by wise guidance you
can wage your war, and in abundance of counselors
there is victory. Wisdom is too high for a fool; in*

I CAN DO ANYTHING IN THE RIGHT PAIR OF SHOES

the gate he does not open his mouth.
Proverbs 24:3-7, ESV

A fool gives full vent to his spirit, but a wise man quietly holds it back.
Proverbs 29:11, ESV

Oh, the depth of the riches and wisdom and knowledge of God! How unsearchable are his judgments and how inscrutable his ways!
Romans 11:33, ESV

The wise of heart will receive commandments, but a babbling fool will come to ruin.
Proverbs 10:8, ESV

For the foolishness of God is wiser than men, and the weakness of God is stronger than men.
1 Corinthians 1:25, ESV

Look carefully then how you walk, not as unwise but as wise, making the best use of the time, because the days are evil.
Ephesians 5:15-16, ESV

For to the one who pleases him God has given wisdom and knowledge and joy, but to the sinner he has given the business of gathering and collecting, only to give to one who pleases God. This also is vanity and a striving after wind.
Ecclesiastes 2:26, ESV

The Collector's Item—Looking for Lessons Along the Way

By insolence comes nothing but strife, but with those who take advice is wisdom.
Proverbs 13:10, ESV

And he said to man, "Behold, the fear of the Lord, that is wisdom, and to turn away from evil is understanding."
Job 28:28, ESV

Wisdom rests in the heart of a man of understanding, but it makes itself known even in the midst of fools.
Proverbs 14:33, ESV

But the wisdom from above is first pure, then peaceable, gentle, open to reason, full of mercy and good fruits, impartial and sincere.
James 3:17, ESV

I will walk in peace by daily seeking wisdom from God and treating lessons learned like a prized collection.

FOURTEEN

Jesus' Shoes—Choosing Peace Every Day

"The real test of the saint is not preaching the gospel, but washing disciples' feet, that is, doing the things that do not count in the actual estimate of men, but count everything in the estimate of God."
—Oswald Chambers, evangelist and teacher[46]

Last but not least, in the list of shoes to acknowledge, are the shoes of Jesus. Following in Jesus' shoes is a great aspiration for anyone, regardless of your view of religion, faith, or God, Jesus walked out the model human life. As someone who believes that Jesus is God who came as a human to live the perfect life that I couldn't live, I believe Jesus died for me so I could walk in peace with God. Jesus gives me a chance to have peace with God and to have a relationship with Him. Jesus is the only person I should seek to model my life after.

Jesus washing the feet of his disciples is one of the best displays of humility. I don't know many people who willingly wash the feet of others, do you? The King of Kings and Lord of Lords washed the feet of his disciples. You may be wondering how this is relevant to putting on the shoes of peace. Putting on shoes of peace, just like washing the disciples' feet, is intentional and involves humility as you ask God to help you do it daily, even moment by moment.

I CAN DO ANYTHING IN THE RIGHT PAIR OF SHOES

Choosing to Walk in Peace is Not Easy

Choosing peace daily involves the things discussed in earlier chapters: dealing with your past, walking with peace in the present, and also planning to walk in it each day in the future. I realize this is not easy, but things that are easy are rarely worth it. Conversely, things that are not easy are almost always worth it.

Putting on the feet of peace each day is essential to prepare for difficult times and walking in a turbulent world. A difficult time could involve hurtful comments from others. As I've mentioned before, I hate when people notice the difference in my legs. I'm sensitive to this, because since I was a little girl, I didn't want my legs to look different, but I can't help it. Don't get me wrong, I'm thankful, and I'm blessed to have come as far as I have in running a marathon, wearing heels, and basically living a life walking around as if nothing was different about my legs or feet. However, when someone notices my legs, I still don't like it.

A couple of years ago, I went to a local chiropractor who was not my normal practitioner. I benefit from monthly chiropractic care because of my hip and back issues. This chiropractor asked about my legs/feet. I never know where this is going next, so I typically hate the question, because it makes me feel like something is wrong with me, which again, I'm working to overcome.

After I told the chiropractor about being born club-footed, he responded, "At least the top half of you is pretty" . . . Yeah; it hurt. It caught me off guard, and I'm typically pretty quick-witted with my responses. However, this was an area of deep hurt for me and something I've dealt with my entire life, so when this man said this to me, I didn't respond. I just finished the appointment, paid, and left. However, after that, I've never returned, nor will I, to that practice. This person has been forgiven, but he will not receive my money any longer.

Jesus' Shoes—Choosing Peace Every Day

People who know me are probably shocked I didn't come back with something, write a letter, or address it in some way. Honestly, I think I was too shocked in the moment to even respond. I wonder if Jesus felt this way when people were hurting Him, misunderstanding Him, mocking Him? He was fully human, after all. My friends and husband were ready to punch this man in the throat, to say the least. However, I dealt with the situation by putting on the shoes of peace.

What Does It Mean to Walk in Peace in a Turbulent World?

The Greek word for peace is eirene. It means rest, quiet, calmness, and tranquility. It is not referring to the absence of turbulence or war. The peace we put on is a part of our armor for the war we engage in with the enemy, each day, and allows us to stand firm and remain unshakeable, regardless of our circumstances. It also enables us with a willingness to be at peace with others.

I'm learning I should try to put on peace daily.

You should know... in the last days there will be very difficult times. For people will be lovers of self, lovers of money, proud, arrogant, abusive, disobedient to their parents, ungrateful, unholy, heartless, unappeasable, slanderous, without self-control, brutal, not loving good, treacherous, reckless, swollen with conceit, lovers of pleasure rather than lovers of God, having the appearance of godliness, but denying its power. Avoid such people.
2 Timothy 3:1, ESV

To truly be like Jesus, we must realize that peace isn't something that simply happens to you; you have to put it on like putting on shoes. Strolling with God each day requires the right attitude and action. Feelings are often misleading and can't always be trusted. Peace can't just be a feeling. It is much like a piece of armor you have to wear. I used to believe peace was a byproduct of life and the choices I made. Now, I choose to put on peace each day.

Follow Jesus' Example

Jesus understood the necessity of putting on the shoes of peace daily. In Genesis, even before Jesus was mentioned by name, feet were used in the foreshadowing of how we would find ultimate peace.

Genesis 3:1-15, ESV, tells the infamous story of how sin entered the world. The serpent was a picture of Satan, the great deceiver, enemy of God, and hater of His creation. This sly, cunning being wanted to destroy everything God loved, so he deceived Adam and Eve in the garden. He whispered lies to them and twisted the truth, just enough for Adam and Eve to question God and turn away from his command. After God addressed Adam and Eve when they sinned, He then said this to the serpent/Satan:

> "Because you have done this,
> Cursed are you more than all the livestock,
> And more than any animal of the field;
> On your belly you shall go,
> And dust you shall eat
> All the days of your life;
> And I will make enemies
> Of you and the woman,
> ***And of your offspring and her Descendant;***
> ***He shall bruise you on the head,***
> ***And you shall bruise Him on the heel.***"

Jesus' Shoes—Choosing Peace Every Day

From the beginning, God created us with free will, and when man chose to go his own way instead of God's, the world was cursed. However, as Scripture states in Genesis 3:15, God promises that the offspring of the woman will bruise the head of the serpent. The image here is of a foot crushing a snake. He could have used a hand or for that matter a butt, lol. I probably have a lot more force in my fist or butt than I do with my pitiful feet, but I digress. God basically promised here to stomp on Satan.

Of course, the serpent does bruise God on the heel, which is symbolic of Jesus having to die for our sin. He was wounded for our transgressions and bruised for our iniquities as scripture says in Isaiah 53:5.

A heel is representative of the serpent being dealt with by God. The offspring of the woman is Jesus, who Christians believe is God in the form of a man. Jesus is called the son of God, but He is a part of the one true and triune (three in one) God. He came willingly to lay down his life for humans, for us, so we can live in eternity and have communion with God forever. Before Jesus came, Isaiah (9:6, ESV) prophesied, "For to us a child is born, to us a son is given, and the government will be on his shoulders. And he will be called Wonderful Counselor, Mighty God, Everlasting Father, Prince of Peace." We have peace when we accept Jesus as our Lord and Savior, acknowledging he died in our place. We are right with God because of our faith in Jesus. This brings us peace with God!

Think about the fact that to be a Prince, you have to have the bloodline of the royal line. Jesus, as the Prince of Peace, means peace is in his DNA; He is peace! As the Prince of Peace, Jesus is the only one who can truly restore our relationship with God, give us the right to go to heaven, and help us to have peace in our daily lives.

As the Prince of Peace took off his heavenly royalty and entered the world, he didn't stop being peace. Ephesians

2:17-19, ESV, says, "He came and preached peace to you who were far away and peace to those who were near. For through Him we both have access to the Father by one Spirit. Therefore you are no longer strangers and foreigners, but fellow citizens with the saints and members of God's household!" When we have access to the Father, and we choose to put on peace daily, we can then live as God intended us to live, even in a broken world. Those of us who are co-heirs with Christ should follow the example of the Prince of Peace by living in peace and preaching it to those far and near.

The Jewish word for peace is Shalom, but it means much more than what English speakers may interpret as peace. It is a Hebrew word that means complete wholeness. Peace, in a sense, describes the original way God intended the world to be for humans. When man sinned, peace or shalom was broken, and the world was no longer as God intended. Thankfully, when Jesus came as the Prince of Peace, he restored Shalom! Jesus was our kinsman redeemer, the only rightful person who could redeem relationships and give us a chance to live eternally, in peace, as we were intended to in the beginning!

The peace Jesus offers not only secures our destiny with God; it can also flow into our lives daily! Galatians 6:15-16 (my paraphrase) states we are a new creation in Christ Jesus, and if we follow this, peace (complete wholeness) and mercy will be the result!

Be Intentional. Put It On.

Peace is something we must intentionally choose to walk in daily. If we put on the shoes of peace, we can stand strong against the enemy. The shoes of peace that we are taught to put on daily in Ephesians 6, prepare us for battle with the enemy. The shoes are to help us stand firm so we can't be struck down when the enemy attacks.

Stop for a moment and close your eyes. Picture yourself putting on the peace of God as shoes. Now, imagine yourself walking out each action today, with confidence, as you live the way God intends you to. What does it look like? Do you hold your head high? Do you notice things you haven't before? Are you prepared for great things to happen? Are you able to go to battle the way God wants when frustrations come your way?

I realize, at this point, you may still be asking, "So what does this look like practically?" Let's review some spiritual disciplines.

Finding Peace through Spiritual Disciplines

Inward or Personal Disciplines: Memorizing Scripture, Meditating on God's Word, Fasting, Prayer

Memorizing Scripture:

If you need peace for _____, memorize the following scripture:

- **Stress about the world**: John 16:33, ESV "I have said these things to you, that in me you may have peace. In the world you will have tribulation. But take heart; I have overcome the world."

- **Safety/life concerns**: Psalm 4:8, ESV "In peace I will both lie down and sleep; for you alone, O Lord, make me dwell in safety."

- **Overcoming fear**: Daniel 10:19, ESV "And he said, 'O man greatly loved, fear not, peace be with you; be strong and of good courage.' And as he spoke to me, I was strengthened and said, 'Let my lord speak, for you have strengthened me.' "

- **Letting peace rule**: Colossians 3:1, ESV "Let the peace of Christ rule in your hearts, since as members of one body you were called to peace. And be thankful."

- **Encouragement to walk in peace**: Isaiah 52:7. ESV "How beautiful on the mountains are the feet of those who bring good news, who proclaim peace, who bring good tidings, who proclaim salvation, who say to Zion, 'Your God reigns!' "

- **Hope for the future**: Proverbs 3:16-18. ESV "Long life is in her right hand; in her left hand are riches and honor. Her ways are ways of pleasantness, and all her paths are peace. She is a tree of life to those who lay hold of her; those who hold her fast are called blessed."

- **Troubled heart**: John 14:27, ESV "Peace I leave with you; my peace I give to you. Not as the world gives do I give to you. Let not your hearts be troubled, neither let them be afraid."

- **Discovering what matters most**: Romans 14:17, ESV "For the kingdom of God is not a matter of eating and drinking but of righteousness and peace and joy in the Holy Spirit."

- **Guarding your heart and mind**: Philippians 4:7, ESV "And the peace of God, which surpasses all understanding, will guard your hearts and your minds in Christ Jesus."

- **Feeling overwhelmed or empty**: Jude 1:2, ESV "May

mercy, peace, and love be multiplied to you."

Meditating on God's word

Make meditation a part of your daily practice for putting on peace and walking in it. You can use this book, make up your own, or use an app on your device such as ABIDE (my personal favorite).

Meditation should also include some form of Bible study. My personal favorite method of study is Kay Arthurs' Inductive Bible Study method. She teaches you how to study, and this method has truly been the conduit for me to fall in love with God's word! Don't say Bible study is too hard or boring or you don't have enough time. It can be exciting and exhilarating. We make time to do the things we want to do. That is truly the bottom line. There are also plenty of resources available these days, making Bible study easy. So, we have no excuses.

Fasting

Fasting is discussed throughout the Bible. Isaiah said, "Isn't this the fast I choose: To break the chains of wickedness, to untie the ropes of the yoke, to set the oppressed free, and to tear off every yoke" (Isaiah 58:6. ESV)? Biblical fasting is truly about acknowledging Christ as Lord and realizing you love God more than anything else. Fasting can be from food, technology, words, music, etc. I recommend starting with something that you depend on (i.e. caffeine), but it is okay to start slowly if you've never done it before. For example, try fasting by only drinking one cup of coffee a day instead of four (like me).

At times, I've fasted from social media, non-Christian music, certain types of beverages, food for a day or so at a time, etc. Pray and ask God to reveal to you what He wants you to fast from. Give it a try, and see how it can help you walk in peace.

Prayer

Prayer, unlike meditation, is something you can do all day long. Prayer is our way of communicating with God. It can be done in solitude or driving in your car. It is talking to God. Look to Jesus for His model, if you are unsure how to begin. The Lord's prayer is the model prayer and how Jesus taught the disciples to pray.

"This, then, is how you should pray:
"Our Father in heaven, hallowed be your name, your kingdom come, your will be done, on earth as it is in heaven. Give us today our daily bread. And forgive us our debts, as we also have forgiven our debtors. And lead us not into temptation, but deliver us from the evil one."
Matthew 6:9-13, ESV

Here is how I try to model the Lord's prayer: I start praying by being thankful, then I pray for God's will to be done. Next, I pray for what I need for that moment or day, ask for forgiveness, and that I will be forgiving of others. I end by asking God to help me in times of temptation and to fight the devil. However, at times, when I can't find my focus, in my prayer time, I may cry out to God or sit and laugh with God. Our Father loves talking to us and hearing our prayers. He wants to talk to you every day, all day!

Solitude

Taking time away to rest and seek is also important

for walking in peace. Having a daily, weekly, and occasionally longer period to focus on solitude will bring more peace to your life. Here are a few things to consider in seeking solitude:

Daily: Find a peaceful place in your home or area where you live. You can take a walk without your phone. Consider walking barefoot in the grass. It is called *grounding* and is an up-and-coming technique proven to improve mood, decrease inflammation in your body, and more. I think it is focusing your mind and body on God's creation and His goodness.

Weekly: Take a nap. Enjoy a walk in the woods.

Monthly, quarterly, or yearly times away: Go on a peaceful trip! Be intentional about your time on the trip, and spend time with God. Enjoy quiet time. Explore a new peaceful place.

Plan time to be alone in the Lord's presence and relax.

Outward or Others-focused Spiritual Disciplines: Serving Others, Worshiping/Celebrating God with Others, and Seeking Biblical Counseling/Wisdom and Confession

Serving Others

We were created to serve others. I dare you to try serving others, and see how it makes you feel and think. It is a way to bring more peace into your daily walk.

Worshiping and Celebrating with Others

Worshiping God alongside community is something He told us to do. Hebrews 10-24-25, ESV, says, "And let us consider how to spur one another on to love and good deeds. Let us not neglect meeting together, as some have made a habit, but let us encourage one another, and all the more as you see the Day approaching."

I realize many, including myself, have been hurt in church. Church is full of broken people/sinners. Therefore, if you've been in a church long enough, you've likely experienced hurt from others. However, God desires for us to try to work out differences and keep spurring one another on to love and good deeds. Find a place where you can serve in the season of life you are in. Although you may experience hurt, you can also experience healing from the love of others as you serve together as a church family.

Seek guidance from Biblical counselors, as needed, and practice confession.

Did you know it is actually Biblical to seek Godly counsel? Proverbs 15:22, ESV states, "Without counsel plans fail, but with many advisers they succeed, and Proverbs 24:6, ESV, states, "For by wise guidance you can wage your war, and in abundance of counselors there is victory." At times, you may need to seek counseling to help you walk in peace. It doesn't mean you are crazy. It actually suggests the opposite. Seeking Godly counsel shows you want to be mentally well and healthy. When I'm asked, "Do you see a bunch of crazy people?" I respond, "No; crazy people never seek counseling. I see the people who are trying to deal with the crazy in their lives." So, give counseling a try!

Finally, consider creating and saying a daily mantra, so you can plan for peace each day. Do it before you get out of bed!

Here is an example:

Today I will walk in peace at all costs. I will remember God's goodness and be thankful for His word, as I hide it in my heart. His joy will overflow in my life to others, as I walk in peace.

In conclusion, I pray the following two verses over you:

> *Now may the God of peace, who through the blood of the eternal covenant brought back from the dead our Lord Jesus, that great Shepherd of the sheep, equip you with everything good for doing his will, and may he work in us what is pleasing to him, through Jesus Christ, to whom be glory for ever and ever. Amen.*
> Hebrews 13:20-21, ESV

> *I have told you these things, so that in me you may have peace. In this world you will have trouble. But take heart! I have overcome the world.*
> John 16:33, ESV

> *And the God of peace will soon crush Satan under your feet! (Feel free to shout praise here!)*
> Romans 16:20, ESV

I will walk in peace by choosing to put on Jesus' shoes, the shoes of peace, which surpasses all understanding, and will guard my heart and my mind in Christ Jesus.

Notes

1. McCarthy, Cormac. All the Pretty Horses. London, UK: Picador Collection, 2022.
2. "Mary Johnson and Oshea Israel," The Forgiveness Project, February 25, 2021, accessed August 29, 2022, https://www.theforgivenessproject.com/stories-library/mary-johnson-oshea-israel/.
3. Solomon, Andrew. The Noonday Demon: An Atlas of Depression. New York: Scribner Classics, 2015.
4. Plath, Sylvia. The Bell Jar. New York: Harper & Row, 1971.
5. Merriam-Webster, s.v. "Patent," accessed August 28, 2022, https://www.merriam-webster.com/dictionary/patent.
6. "Imprinting." Good Therapy, August 10, 2015, accessed August 29, 2022, https://www.goodtherapy.org/blog/psychpedia/imprinting.
7.
8. Kaufman, Susanna. "The 8 Phases of EMDR Therapy: Corner Canyon Health Centers." Emdria, Corner Canyon HC, August 11, 2022. https://cornercanyonhc.com/blog/8-phases-emdr-therapy/.
9. "Noortje De Bijl Quotes." Goodreads. Accessed August 29, 2022. https://www.goodreads.com/author/quotes/15075628.Noortje_de_Bijl.

10. Webber, Rebecca. "The Comparison Trap." Psychology Today. Sussex Publishers. Accessed August 29, 2022. https://www.psychologytoday.com/us/articles/201711/the-comparison-trap.
11. "Top 25 Quotes by Callie Khouri: A-Z Quotes." AZ Quotes. Accessed August 29, 2022. https://www.azquotes.com/author/26898-Callie_Khouri.
12. Bardwick, Judith M. Danger in the Comfort Zone: From Boardroom to Mailroom--How to Break the Entitlement Habit That's Killing American Business. New York, NY: Amacom, American Management Association, 1998.
13. "The Innocents Abroad / Roughing It by Mark Twain." Goodreads. Goodreads, December 1, 1984. https://www.goodreads.com/book/show/307844.The_Innocents_Abroad_Roughing_It.
14. Oliver Page, MD. "How to Leave Your Comfort Zone and Enter Your 'Growth Zone'." PositivePsychology.com, July 23, 2022. https://positivepsychology.com/comfort-zone/.
15. "Manolo Blahnik Quotes." BrainyQuote. Xplore. Accessed August 29, 2022. https://www.brainyquote.com/quotes/manolo_blahnik_474773.
16. Gonzalez, Heidi. "Unplanned Pregnancy: Famous Adopted People Birth Parents." Unplanned Pregnancy | Famous Adopted People Birth Parents, June 10, 2020. https://afth.org/famous-people-unplanned-pregnancy/
17. "Groupthink." Encyclopædia Britannica. Encyclopædia Britannica, inc. Accessed August 29, 2022. https://www.britannica.com/science/groupthink.
18. Teitel, Amy Shira. "What Caused the Challenger Disaster?" History.com. A&E Television Networks, January 25, 2018. https://www.history.com/news/how-the-challenger-disaster-changed-nasa.

19. Gessen, Masha. "What HBO's 'Chernobyl' Got Right, and What It Got Terribly Wrong." The New Yorker, June 4, 2019. https://www.newyorker.com/news/our-columnists/what-hbos-chernobyl-got-right-and-what-it-got-terribly-wrong.
20. S, Pangambam. "The Beauty of Conflict: Clair Canfield (Full Transcript)." The Singju Post, April 11, 2020. https://singjupost.com/the-beauty-of-conflict-clair-canfield-full-transcript/.
21. Odell, Amy. "Spring Fashion 2010 - Q&A with 'Vogue' Nippon Fashion Director Anna Dello Russo on Her from-the-Runway Looks -- New York Magazine - Nymag." New York Magazine. New York Magazine, February 10, 2010. https://nymag.com/fashion/10/spring/63803/.
22. "The Pebble in Your Shoe," Inside Watch Africa, February 10, 2021, accessed August 29, 2022, https://insidewatchafrica.org/2021/02/the-pebble-in-your-shoe/.
23. Sauer VJ, Eimler SC, Maafi S, Pietrek M, Krämer NC. The phantom in my pocket: Determinants of phantom phone sensations. Mobile Media & Communication. 2015;3(3):293-316. doi:10.1177/2050157914562656.
24. Sauer VJ, Eimler SC, Maafi S, Pietrek M, Krämer NC. The phantom in my pocket: Determinants of phantom phone sensations. Mobile Media & Communication. 2015;3(3):293-316. doi:10.1177/2050157914562656.
25. Trevor Haynes, "Dopamine, Smartphones & You: A Battle for Your Time." Harvard University, February 4, 2021, accessed August 22, 2022, https://sitn.hms.harvard.edu/flash/2018/dopamine-smartphones-battle-time/.
26. Tom Falkenstein, MA, "How to Deal with Overstimulation." Psychology Today. October 17, 2019, accessed August 29, 2022, https://www.psychologytoday.com/us/blog/

the-highly-sensitive-man/201910/how-deal-overstimulation.

27. "Opioids." National Institute of Health, U.S. Department of Health and Human Services, July 18, 2022, accessed August 29, 2022, https://nida.nih.gov/research-topics/opioids.

28. Lewis, CS. The Great Divorce: A Dream. London: Harper Collins, 2002.

29. We Heart It | Get lost in what you love. "So Many Shoes and Only Two Feet. (Sarah Jessica Parker, as Carrie Bradshaw, Twitter)." We Heart It, August 27, 2022. https://weheartit.com/entry/314099264.

30. Putai Jin, "Stress and Learning," Springer US, January 1, 1970, accessed August 29, 2023, https://link.springer.com/referenceworkentry/10.1007%2F978-1-4419-1428-6_203.

31. "Chronic Stress Puts Your Health at Risk," Mayo Foundation for Medical Education and Research, July 8, 2021, accessed August 29, 2022, https://www.mayoclinic.org/healthy-lifestyle/stress-management/in-depth/stress/art-20046037.

32. "New APA Poll Shows Sustained Anxiety among Americans; More than Half of Parents Are Concerned About," American Psychiatric Association, May 2, 2021, accessed August 29, 2022, https://www.psychiatry.org/newsroom/news-releases/new-apa-poll-shows-sustained-anxiety-among-americans-more-than-half-of-parents-are-concerned-about-the-mental-well-being-of-their-children.

33. Vicente Javier Clemente-Suárez, José Juan Robles-Pérez, Jesús Fernández-Lucas, "Psychophysiological Response in Parachute Jumps, the Effect of Experience and Type of Jump," National Library of Medicine, June 13, 2017, accessed August 29, 2022, https://pubmed.ncbi.nlm.nih.

gov/28619292/.

34. "Bible Commentary - Matthew Henry Consise," biblestudytools.com, 1706, accessed August 29, 2022, https://www.biblestudytools.com/commentaries/matthew-henry-concise/.

35. "Selfish Quotes Quotes (35 Quotes)," Goodreads, accessed August 29, 2022, https://www.goodreads.com/quotes/tag/selfish-quotes.

36. Jim Teague, "Finding Freedom by Forgetting Self," First Presbyterian Church of Evanston, 2023, accessed August 29, 2022, https://firstpresevanston.org/2022/03/finding-freedom-by-forgetting-self/.

37. Sally Holmes, "The Story Behind Michael Jordan's Air Jordans," Marie Claire Magazine, May 18, 2020, accessed August 29, 2022, https://www.marieclaire.com/fashion/a32555197/air-jordans-history/.

38. Lauren Slater, "The Trouble with Self-Esteem," The New York Times, February 3, 2002, accessed August 29, 2023, https://www.nytimes.com/2002/02/03/magazine/the-trouble-with-self-esteem.html.

39. CS Lewis, The Great Divorce: A Dream, (New York, NY: Harper Collins, 1980), 121-22.

40. "The Nobel Peace Prize 1979," The Nobel Prize, 2023, accessed August 29, 2022, https://www.nobelprize.org/prizes/peace/1979/teresa/biographical/.

41. Zeke J. Miller, "Martin Luther King Jr.. and Lessons from Peaceful Protests," Time, January 12, 2018, accessed Auguest 29, 2023, https://time.com/5101740/martin-luther-king-peaceful-protests-lessons/.

42. "Biography," RUTH BELL GRAHAM, Billy Graham Evangelistic Association, October 31, 2019, accessed Au-

gust 29, 2002, https://ruthbellgrahammemorial.org/biography/.

43. "Here's the Real Reason Why Louboutin Shoes Are Red on the Bottom," Vision Viral, March 16, 2021, accessed August 29, 2022, https://visionviral.com/heres-the-real-reason-why-louboutin-shoes-are-red-on-the-bottom/.

44. Oxford Reference. (Oxford: Oxford University Press, 2023), s.v. "Confirmation bias."

45. Kevin Payne. "How to Invest in Sneakers (Yes, We Said Sneakers)," FinanceBuzz, February 6, 2023, accessed by August 25, 2022, https://financebuzz.com/how-to-invest-in-sneakers.

46. Chambers, Oswald. My Utmost for His Highest: Selections for the Year. Uhrichsville, OH: Barbour & Co., 2000.

Acknowledgements

First of all, thank YOU for investing time, energy and maybe money in this book by reading it. My prayer is that you learn something and that you are truly blessed by God's goodness through reading.

I would like to acknowledge the immeasurable debt I owe to my parents for raising me to know Jehovah God of the Bible. Their patience in allowing me to ask the tough questions encouraged a love of learning and studying the deep things which didn't steer me away from faith but rather drove me deeper. This led to a desire to write about some of my story in this book.

Thank you to my sisters, family members, friends, mentors, pastors, and others who have been a part of my story and for believing in me to bring this book to fruition. I also recognize Liz Hughes, Jessica Russell and all those at United House Publishing for their hard work on this book.

Finally, this book would not have been able to be completed without the undying love and support of my husband Donnie, who sacrificially gave me time, such a valuable commodity, to write while he took care of our two boys. Many say that behind a good man is a good woman, but I argue that the converse it also true. Behind this woman is an extremely self-sacrificing husband who always pushes me to be the best

I can by never trying to hold me back, never competing with, or feeling threatened by my independence. He has truly sharpened me as iron sharpens iron.

About the Author

Dr. Natalie Atwell is a Licensed Clinical Mental Health Counselor, Educator and Consultant. She runs a private counseling practice in the Charlotte, NC metro area and teaches graduate counseling courses at Liberty University. Dr. Atwell speaks at businesses and churches upon request and considers it an honor to have a front-row seat in the healing of others through counseling. Hopeful to share the joy and peace of a relationship with Jesus and others, she seeks to contribute to a wider audience through writing. Likely though her own struggles with shoes due to a birth defect, she has come to love shoes and since God thought his word talks about shoes of peace, it seemed to be a perfect fit for her first book.

In her practice, Dr. Atwell sees the need daily for people to have peace in this crazy world, a peace which can only come when they deal with their past, focus on the present, and prepare for their future. In I Can Do Anything in the Right Pair of Shoes, Dr. Atwell welcomes you to laugh and be encouraged as she invites you into her journey of learning how to put on the shoes of peace, not peace from the world but the peace that only Jesus offers.

www.ingramcontent.com/pod-product-compliance
Lightning Source LLC
Chambersburg PA
CBHW070135080526
44586CB00015B/1698